Cameron Wislang is 26 years old and lives on the Kāpiti Coast, near Wellington, with his wife, Kaitlyn, and two girls, Ivy (who thinks money just comes out of the machine in the wall) and Maisie (who thinks grown-ups just go to work to see their friends).

Helping everyday people get ahead is what makes Cameron tick. He has helped people with severe mental illnesses get into work, coaching them on the money that will soon be coming in. He sits down with young people to help them come up with budgets, save for their goals and pull themselves out of debt.

While on a constant learning journey himself, Cameron thinks he knows a thing or two about making and managing money. From a young age he has been switched on to how the world revolves around money and has achieved outstanding personal results.

BUDGET LIKE A LEGEND

HOT TIPS FROM A GUY WHO'S BEEN THERE

CAMERON WISLANG

HarperCollins*Publishers*

HarperCollins*Publishers*
Australia • Brazil • Canada • France • Germany • Holland • India
Italy • Japan • Mexico • New Zealand • Poland • Spain • Sweden
Switzerland • United Kingdom • United States of America

First published in 2024
by HarperCollins*Publishers* (New Zealand) Limited
Unit D1, 63 Apollo Drive, Rosedale, Auckland 0632, New Zealand
harpercollins.co.nz

A catalogue record for this book is available from the National Library of New
Zealand

ISBN 978 1 7755 4248 3 (pbk)
ISBN 978 1 7754 9279 5 (ebook)

Cover design by Mietta Yans, HarperCollins Design Studio
Cover images by istockphoto.com and shutterstock.com
Typeset in Adobe Garamond Pro by Kirby Jones
Printed and bound in Australia by McPherson's Printing Group

To my girls.
Financial literacy is one of the best things I can give you.
Use it and conquer your dreams.

x

Contents

Hello!

Well done you for picking up this FABULOUS book (if I do say so myself). It truly is a masterpiece. Okay, maybe not a masterpiece, but hopefully something that will be somewhat helpful to you. I, like many others, think that I know a thing or two when it comes to money and how to be smart with it to achieve your goals. The reality is that I probably don't know as much as I think I do, but, hey, you are reading now, so you might as well see if there is anything worth your time in here.

Man, what a good way to start a book. SELF-CONFIDENCE, people! My words are screaming it, are they not? ☺

My name's Cameron, and I'm a super-nerd when it comes to numbers. I love a good spreadsheet. I have been writing budgets for as long as I can remember. I love taking someone's figures and breaking them down into a colour-coded and interactive spreadsheet to help them set goals and realise their potential. Hot, right?

What I've learnt from all this, I want to share with you: this whole budgeting, sorting out your money thing – whatever you want to call it – is not impossible. It is not something only smart, educated or lucky people can do. It is something that every single person can accomplish. You might need a helping hand or two along the way (that's why you've picked up this book, right?) but I believe in you. You have just as much ability as anyone else to do this.

'Is it too late for me to start?'

There is no age limit for financial literacy.

Start where you are.

There is always space for you at the table.

I am not a financial advisor or registered with any sort of financial place of any kind; I am just a guy who has been there, done that. Or is doing that, I should say. Before you ask, no, I haven't had help from my parents. (No, Daddy didn't buy me a Mercedes for my eighteenth birthday. No, I didn't start off with Donald Trump's humble beginnings: 'a small loan of one million dollars'.) When my wife, Kaitlyn, and I met, we were broke AF. Now we own our house and are living pretty comfortably. We're not where we aspire to be yet, but we are well on our way.

When I hear people say 'It's too expensive' or 'I don't have enough money' or 'I can't afford it', it doesn't quite compute in my head. If that's you, this book is here to get you thinking, 'How can I get that? What do I need to do to make that my reality?'

Young people (and, if you've read this far, I'm guessing you don't yet have grandkids; if you do, hey, Nan/Pop, welcome!) have more energy than they ever will, more resiliency, fewer financial commitments and far less risk – it's the perfect time in life to embrace working hard and setting yourself up financially.

Financial literacy isn't just for 'smart' people.
It's a skill you can learn, just like anything else.
Believe in yourself.
You're more capable than you think.

This book is about your money – how to use it and how to save it. I'll guide you through writing a budget and setting some financial goals. I'm not going to tell you how to get rich quickly or send you on a wild goose chase with far-fetched ideas and complicated theories. I'm going to talk about money the way you would – not a banker or law professor. (I am certainly neither of those things.)

By the end of this book, you will feel more comfortable talking about money, you'll be confident in managing it, and you'll be looking for ways to learn more about it. Improving your financial literacy, aka learning about money, is one of the best things you can do for yourself and your future. It'll give you the tools you need to seek out new ways to manage and invest your money, and new perspectives on what works best. If we don't stop learning, we'll never stop growing and becoming better versions of ourselves – and that's true of our money-minded selves too.

Without any more fluff, let's get on with it.

'Getting ahead' with money comes down to three things:

1) what you spend
2) what you earn
3) your financial literacy.

Don't brush off the last point. It's crucial.

Chapter 1

Budgets

Writing a budget

Everyone needs a budget. It doesn't matter if you earn one dollar or a million dollars each year – you need a budget. Why? It's simple, really: if you don't understand where your money is going, or how much you have to spend on something, then you are likely to overspend and land yourself in debt. People live beyond their means all the time without realising it. Recently a close friend of mine told me they'd discovered they were spending 150% more at the supermarket each week than they'd thought – they hadn't realised how much all the small shops add up! Why do you think some Lotto winners go broke? They get a windfall and feel like they can spend at a high level for a long time – they don't realise how quickly the money disappears.

Budgets can seem scary, boring or downright confusing, but they don't need to be. A budget is like a plan for your money: what money comes in and what goes out? It breaks it all down and gives you the power to know where all your money disappears after payday!

It's easy to make your own budget.

- First, how much money do you get? This should include any income – your pay from work, benefits, grants, gifts or allowances. Weekly, fortnightly or monthly – include it all. The only thing you might not add in here is money you don't receive regularly, like dividends from investments, and that doesn't add to your available everyday money.

- Second, how much money do you spend on essentials? This is all the money that you spend on bills and other expenses. Go through your bank statements and take a good look – don't miss anything out. For things that you spend a different amount on each week, like groceries, total the cost up for six weeks and divide by six to calculate the weekly average. Make sure you add in one-off and occasional costs, too, like the warrant of fitness (WoF) for your car. For these, take the total yearly cost and divide it by 52 (to get the cost per week), 26 (the cost per fortnight) or 12 (the cost per month). A good way to get a full picture of how much you are really spending is to record your spending over three months and calculate the averages.

- Third, what's left over? Do you have any money remaining after everything's come in and gone out? If you do, we're going to split this money up into different categories.

Start by filling out the table on the following page. If you have money coming in weekly, use your weekly totals; if money comes in fortnightly, use fortnightly totals; and if it comes in monthly, use monthly totals. A good thing to remember is that unless you are a contractor (more on this in Chapter 4), your KiwiSaver and tax will automatically come out of your pay before you receive it.

How did you go? Did a little vomit come up in your mouth when you saw how expensive it is to be an adult? Yeah … me too.

This table includes your typical expenses but not everything. Make sure you go through your bank statements to see if there's anything you've forgotten (think takeaway coffees, haircuts, gym membership and so on).

If you want your budget to look a little more structured, you could sort your expenses into groups: fixed and non-fixed. Fixed costs are bills that come in at the same price no matter what. Things like rent, internet and insurance are fixed costs. Non-fixed costs are bills that tend to go up and down depending on your week, like groceries, clothing, petrol and so on. I group my expenses like this because I like to colour-code shit and pretend I'm super smart, but you do you.

My income and expenses

INCOME	☐ Weekly ☐ Fortnightly ☐ Monthly
Wages, salary, benefit, etc.	$
Additional income (grants, gifts, allowances, etc.)	$
Total income	**$**
EXPENSES	
Rent/mortgage	$
Rates	$
Water	$
Power/gas	$
Internet	$
Phone	$
Insurance (home, car, contents, health, life, etc.)	$
Groceries	$
Transport (petrol, public transport, Uber, etc.)	$
Rubbish (bin collection, waste removal, etc.)	$
Childcare	$
Subscriptions (Netflix, Apple Music, etc.)	$
Debt repayments	$
Car maintenance (WoF, registration, etc.)	$
Clothing	$
Medical	$
Donations/gifts/koha	$
Other	$
	$
	$
	$
	$
Total expenses	**$**

Bank accounts

So, I guess you're now wondering where the best place to put your money is if it's not in your hot little fist?

Great question. To answer it, we are going to talk about bank accounts.

Bank accounts are one of those things you need to have. We all use them to spend money and receive money. But did you know that some are better than others? And no, not just because their cards are brighter colours or they have cool adverts. It's often the bank accounts you have never heard about that give you the best deals.

Interestingly, a lot of us will have first learnt about money when we learnt about banks. Do you remember being at school and having a bank come in to hand out deposit-slip books, piggy banks and stickers? It all seemed so cool (to me anyway!). Banks turn up to schools to teach kids how great it is to save. Fast-forward ten years and they are offering you credit cards, overdrafts and loans …

In New Zealand, there are heaps of different banks. Many will charge you fees and give you little or no interest on your savings. And that's not cool for you. If you are with one of the major banks, chances are you are in this boat. But there is hope!

You want the money you earn to make as much interest as possible, and you want to be charged as few fees as possible.

In case you are wondering what interest is – it's magic. It's pretty much like Red Bull for your money. You get paid money for having money. It's that simple.

You want the money you earn to make as much interest as possible, and you want to be charged as few fees as possible. In case you are wondering what interest is – it's magic. It's pretty much like Red Bull for your money. You get paid money for having money. It's that simple.

Not all banks are equal. As I write this, the standard rate for one major bank's savings account is 1.1% p.a. (p.a. means 'per annum', or per year). They also only offer one free withdrawal per month, and they charge $5 for every withdrawal after that. Say you have $1,000 in this account. In one year, you will earn a whole $11.06 in interest. And if you take out money just twice a month, you will be charged $5 each month to do so. This means you'll pay $60 in fees across the year!

But, if you don't make more than one withdrawal a month, the bank will reward you with an interest rate of 4.25% p.a., giving you interest of $43.34 a year when compounding monthly.

In comparison, a smaller, less-well-known bank offers 4.6% p.a. on their standard savings account. If you have $1,000 in there, compounding monthly, you will earn $46.98 a year. There are no fees and no penalties if you withdraw money. And, if you give them 32 days' notice that you want to make a withdrawal, they will reward you with an interest rate of 5.25% p.a., compounding monthly, giving you interest of $53.78 per year. Still with no fees.

Do you get my drift?

It's time to look at your bank account. A lot of the big banks charge fees on everyday accounts (around $5 a month). This is a cost you can avoid. Find a bank that has no fees.

Most banks give you stuff-all interest on your money. This is another downer you can dodge. Find a bank that gives you the most amount of interest with zero fees.

In New Zealand, Heartland Bank and TSB are two of the banks that offer higher interest rates and lower, or no, fees. Do your own checking and find the accounts that work best for you. With most banks, you can open an account online or in-store. There is no limit to how many different banks you can be with. Kaitlyn and I are with three.

why our money is split across three different banks

Bank #1

Our mortgage with our mortgage broker is through this bank. We have two accounts (one for our emergency fund + mortgage lump sum, and the other for our bills), and both of these offset our mortgage.

Bank #2

We are with this bank because our main bank doesn't offer debit cards. All of our sinking funds (e.g. car, cats, family and personal spending) are with this bank. We use a debit card for online purchases.

Bank #3

Our third bank is purely for our short-term savings. This is for things like travel or big landscaping work. We chose this bank for our savings accounts because it has zero fees and high interest rates.

It's important to remember that banks make a killing off the money they lend out. Most banks get their money from three main sources:

1. the money their customers deposit (aka your hard-earned cash)
2. the money they borrow from the Reserve Bank
3. the money they earn through overseas investments and markets.

Banks have to pay interest on the money they borrow – mainly to the Reserve Bank but also on the money their customers deposit. (Yes, even though your money is showing in your account, your bank is lending it out – it's how they pay you interest on your savings.)

Banks use the money they get to provide products like mortgages, personal loans, credit cards and other lending. They charge a higher amount of interest on the money they lend to their customers than they pay on the money they have borrowed, and then they pocket the difference. This is how they make a profit. And boy – banks make a lot of profit. In New Zealand, banks have recently been posting record-high profits, despite the cost-of-living crisis and high mortgage rates that are putting people in seriously tight financial positions following record-low rates just a year prior. From October 2022 to the end of March 2023, Bank of New Zealand made an after-tax profit of $805 million – an increase of 13.5% since just the previous six-month period! And – if you think that is a lot – wait until you hear ANZ's. In the same period, ANZ made a cash profit of $1.1 billion. With a B. To put that in perspective, it looks like this: $1,100,000,000. That's just over 16,000 brand-new Tesla Model 3s in six months.

It is important that banks make a profit. We need the income they generate to support our tax system, and if they didn't make a profit, they wouldn't be here. Without banks, it would be pretty bloody hard to get a mortgage! But it seems to me that consumers are definitely footing an overlarge bill for banks to make these huge profits.

So, my point being, go with the bank that charges you the least amount of money, and that will give you the best deal on a mortgage or a savings account. Often, you can also negotiate a deal that is not advertised – all you need to do is ask. They can afford it!

You're not a golden retriever. You don't have to be loyal to your bank.

Structuring your accounts

So, once you have your bank sorted, you are going to want to make a few different accounts.

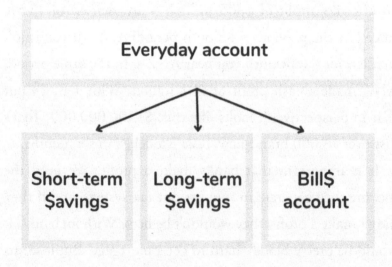

1. An **everyday account** with no fees. All of your money starts by going into this account.

2. A high-interest savings account with no fees. This one is for your **short-term savings**.

3. Another high-interest savings account with no fees for your **long-term savings**. A notice saver – an account where you need to let the bank know in advance when you want the money – is good. Best not to look at this one and just let it grooooow.

4. A **bills account**. Take the total cost of your expenses that you calculated earlier, either weekly, fortnightly or monthly (depending on how often you get paid), and round the number up to the nearest $10. This is the regular amount you need to put into your bills account on payday – it may help to set up an automatic transfer so you don't have to remember to do it each time. All your bill payments should come out of this one account. That way, you don't need to worry about what you need to pay for and when you need to pay for it. You'll need to keep your numbers in mind when buying things like food or petrol – make sure you stick to the number for each expense, and, if you go above it, use your spending money to pay for the excess.

Remember to label your accounts so you know which is which!

Now let's get back to your remainder – the number you calculated by subtracting your bills from your income (if you don't have a remainder, no biggie – you will soon). We are going to break down what to do with that money so that you can make the most of your dollars. Split your total remainder into three chunks: 25% for short-term savings, 50% for long-term savings and 25% for spending.

1. **Short-term savings:** Put aside 25% to save up for smaller items that you need to buy, like a new phone, a laptop or a small holiday – whatever you want that costs a bit extra. Put this money into your short-term savings account.

2. **Long-term savings:** Put the largest chunk of your savings towards the big things – a deposit on a house, a new car, a big holiday. Already have all those things? This is your ticket to paying off your mortgage faster and becoming debt-free. Put this into your long-term savings account.

3. **Spending:** You can spend 25% of your leftover income on whatever you like. Going out, buying treats, having coffee with friends – this money is there to keep you sane. The budgeting world can feel restrictive, and you don't want things to be so hard that you pull the plug – budgeting has got to work for you. Even if you only have $1 left over to spend right

now, don't worry. We're going to make that grow. Your spending money can stay in your everyday account.

Here's an example:

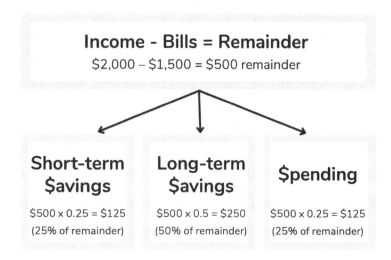

Fill out your figures here:

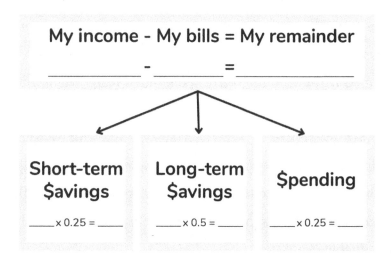

Okay, great. Now you have a budget, and you know what to do with the remainder of your income. You are well on your way to being more zen and less stressy about money. Congrats! Let's keep going.

At the moment, you might find that most of your money is spent on bills and hardly any is saved. If you're keen to change that so you can make it rain later on, start by setting some financial goals. Try not to be unrealistic or out-there crazy. The best place to start? Cut down on spending first, and then focus on how much you want to save.

Adults often have a lot of bills – they'll eat up the large majority of some people's pay, and these people might find themselves living week to week and finding it hard to get ahead. As much as 80% of your pay each week might be spent on bills – and the percentage can get a LOT higher than that! When I first started properly managing my money, I was spending roughly 93% of my pay on bills. So don't be alarmed if the amount you're spending is really high! There is hope.

Start by setting a target. Many books and websites, such as Scott Pape's *The Barefoot Investor*, suggest a target of 60% or less of your pay going towards your bills. This percentage works for me. It might seem hard to reach, but it is doable.

When you reach this target, your income will be divided up like this:

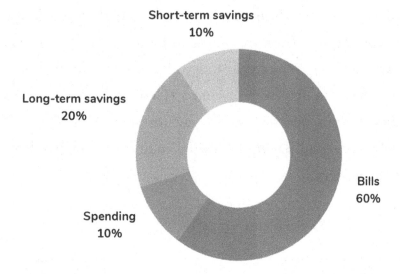

This is one way to manage your money: divide it up by percentages with a goal percentage in mind.

Another way is zero-based budgeting, which is what I do. I have a 'spine' to my budget, based on these percentages, and then I use all the 'fat' around it, too, which means that every dollar of my income is allocated. I don't worry to the point of every last cent, but all my income is allocated to certain bills, savings goals and sinking funds (see below). I don't get too intense about it (I don't verify that every single dollar is spent as planned), but I generally aim towards making sure that every dollar has a purpose.

To get the right balance and make things a bit more achievable, I set up different sinking funds.

Sinking funds

Sinking funds are accounts where you set money aside to pay for something specific, like a bill that you know is coming up. They are meant to be used. Sinking funds can help you avoid the feeling of loss you might get when you have to use your savings. (How many of us have dipped into our savings to pay for something?) It will help you avoid paying for things with buy now, pay later schemes too.

how to set up a sinking fund

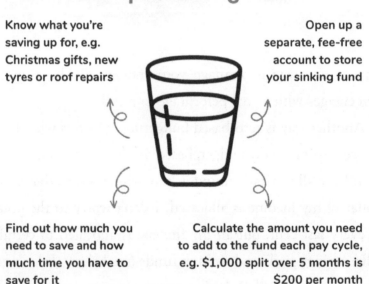

Know what you're saving up for, e.g. Christmas gifts, new tyres or roof repairs

Open up a separate, fee-free account to store your sinking fund

Find out how much you need to save and how much time you have to save for it

Calculate the amount you need to add to the fund each pay cycle, e.g. $1,000 split over 5 months is $200 per month

The following are common sinking funds.

Emergency fund

A nifty little thing to have tucked away in your back pocket is an emergency fund. It can act as your parachute when things turn to shit. Sometimes no matter how much we earn, how smart we save and how diligently we take care of our everyday lives, things go wrong.

why having an emergency fund is vital

You'll still be able to pay all your regular expenses in an emergency

Knowing that you have money available for this purpose alleviates stress

Especially important if you have a serious medical condition, live far away from family, or you own your own home

Avoids adding to current debt or taking out new debt with potentially high interest rates

You won't dip into your personal savings or investments in an emergency

Just the other week I took my car into the mechanic for its regular service and warrant of fitness. When my phone rang later that day, I started picking up my things and getting ready to head over, thinking it was the classic 'Ya car is ready, mate' call. Yeah, nah.

'So we looked under the car and well … we are not letting it leave here. The rear diff is cracked and spilling oil.'

My response: *insert many swear words here*. ☺

The bill came to $4,500 plus the service and WoF fee. Luckily I had an emergency fund that could cover it! When I can, I regularly put chunks of cash – $50 here, $100 there – into an account set aside for reasons just like this. Everything counts, so focus on putting what you can afford in there. Do what you can, and I guarantee it will come in handy one day.

Gifts fund

If you are anything like me, you will forget to add gifts into your budget. At Christmas this can get intense, but gifts pop up at all times of the year – birthdays, engagements, weddings or other celebrations where you feel like contributing something.

Set up a sinking fund to use throughout the year, and regularly contribute small amounts. Estimate how many celebrations will occur across the year and how much you would like to spend on each gift, and then add an extra 20% or so to cover anything unexpected. Break the amount down by each paycheque you'll receive throughout the year to calculate how much to add to your gift fund each time you get paid. If the amount isn't within your means, set an amount that is realistic and that you can regularly add to.

Pets

Pet insurance can cost a lot! We recently got three cats and I was horrified by the amount it would cost to insure them all. Instead, we decided to regularly add to a fund that will hopefully cover all or some of any future costs, like going to the vet or getting a flea treatment (excluding food – this is in our grocery budget). I know that if we end up at the vet, the fund may not cover the whole cost, but at least it's there as a support. We could use our emergency fund as well if needed.

These are just some examples of sinking funds. I like to have my sinking funds in individual accounts so it's nice and clear how much money is in each one. If I was a bit more organised and had a bit more self-restraint, it would make sense for me to have these funds offsetting my mortgage (see page 100), but this is what works for me.

With any budget, many people (including me) will have recommendations of things to try if you ask for advice. Do what works for you. The whole point of budgeting is to make sure you know where your money is going and to be mindful about it. If you have a different way to do this that works for you, then awesome – do that!

Cash stuffing

As mentioned, I use zero-based budgeting with sinking funds and percentage goals as the spine of my budget. I do all this online through bank accounts. Some people might find this method hard because they need something more tangible. If this is you, cash stuffing is a way to use zero-based budgeting with a hands-on component. For any bills that can be paid in cash, small savings and so on, you can make a withdrawal on payday and put allocated amounts for spending and saving into labelled envelopes. Then, until your next payday, you pay for things in each category by using the appropriate envelope. If there is no money left in the envelope, you have to wait until your next payday. Cash stuffing can help build control, and it makes things a lot more real!

Windfalls

People ask me all the time what's the best thing to do if you get a windfall – a large sum of money that is unexpected and doesn't have any conditions attached to it (like there might be if you received a grant for a specific purpose, for example). I am not a financial advisor so I am not going to tell you what to do, but I will tell you about windfalls I have received and what I would do now if I got one.

One of my first jobs when I left home was in corporate recruitment. I was being paid the tiniest amount over minimum wage and working hard for it. At the end of each month, if the team had reached a certain target, we would all get a bonus. This bonus was often equivalent to a week's wage, so in no way small change for us. It was money that came in fairly regularly, but it was uncertain enough that it couldn't be relied on to cover bills, so I didn't include it in my budget. At this time, I didn't save or invest my money – I just spent it all. However, if I HAD saved and invested it, with a modest return rate of about 6% I would now likely have just over $27,000 in that investment, and 33% of that would have been interest generated over seven years. Instead I have nothing to show for it.

When I started my home-ownership journey, I used windfalls to invest in renovations on my home, which led to excellent returns (more on this in Chapter 7).

The problem with windfalls is that they are often just enough money to get rid of an issue. For example, you might get a windfall of $5,000, which is a great amount of money, but you might also have a pressing need that sucks all that money up – maybe you need work done on your car or a kid needs braces or you have overdue bills that have been racking up. I get it – it happens! And it can be so disheartening to see that money, in effect, disappear.

But you can set yourself up so you're ready for a windfall.

The first step is to prioritise your money management. Make sure that you have an emergency fund and a balanced budget. Then, when a windfall comes along, you don't *need* to use it for an emergency expense.

Second: make a plan. That's what I did when I received a back payment from work. I knew that I would be getting a decent amount, so I planned how much of the money I would use for my wants (30%) and how much I would keep aside for my financial goals (70%). I put this 70% into a separate account to help pay a lump sum on my mortgage. Planning helped me resist the temptation to blow it all, especially without realising it – which is so easy to do. Try it next time you receive a windfall and watch how it changes the impact the money can have.

Winning a large amount of money also falls into the windfall category. When people win large amounts of money, they often blow a lot of it without really understanding how or why this happens. The best thing to do? Meet with a financial advisor *before* the money comes in and make a solid plan that results in the money having the best impact on your life. This is especially important if it is a life-changing sum of money. With good planning it could last generations; with poor planning it could be gone within months.

Chapter 2

Reduce your expenses

Let's be honest, a lot of budgeting comes down to, and relies on, reducing expenses. There are a few ways to reduce your expenses that are pretty obvious, and some that most people don't realise are an option. Let's go through them.

Some bills are fixed, like rent. We usually can't change fixed costs too much. But, in the case of rent, you could look into:

- having flatmates
- renting a room out on a short-term basis using a platform like Airbnb
- renting somewhere smaller
- living with family
- boarding (this can be a win–win for elderly people who want company!).

Other fixed bills we normally can't change too much are things like:

- car maintenance
- petrol
- rates
- water.

Plan ahead for bigger costs like car maintenance, and have a small amount regularly going into your bills account (or a sinking fund) to cover the cost without stressing when the time comes.

what living within your means looks like

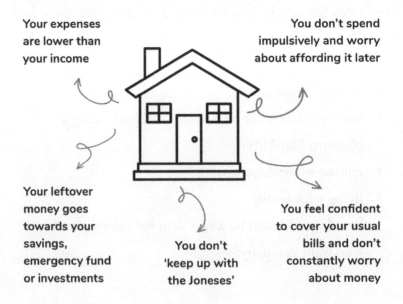

Your expenses are lower than your income

You don't spend impulsively and worry about affording it later

Your leftover money goes towards your savings, emergency fund or investments

You don't 'keep up with the Joneses'

You feel confident to cover your usual bills and don't constantly worry about money

There may be other things you cannot change and that's okay. The golden rule is to use as little as possible, and to live within your means.

Now let's delve into the bills that you CAN change. There are a lot, actually! We'll start with insurance.

Insurance

There are a few different types of insurance, but here are the main ones:

- house
- contents (household items and personal possessions)
- car
- health
- life
- pet.

How do you know which insurances you need and which ones you don't? First off, I am not going to tell you to get or not get insurance. All I want to do is help you weigh it all up. Check in with an insurance broker once you have done your research.

A good rule to follow is to only have insurance for something if you can't otherwise afford to cover the cost if things go wrong. You might be thinking, 'Well, DUH! Why else would I even have insurance?'

And you're right … but hear me out.

If you have health insurance, I want you to think about it. Do you really need it? We live in New Zealand (if you don't, sucks for you, sorry), a country that in comparison to others has a very good health system. When we are sick or injured, we can receive quick, reliable and free services to support us most of the time. We don't need to book into private hospitals for every little thing. Health insurance can be expensive. Humans are, by nature, quite medically needy, so insurance companies don't want to risk having low-cost premiums if someone is likely to use their health insurance a lot.

Weigh it up. Are you someone who needs a lot of treatments that are not covered by the public health system? Are you at risk of a medical condition that is not covered by the system? Would having health insurance, just in case, give you peace of mind and help you sleep better at night? If so, health insurance is probably a smart idea for you. But, if you are normally a healthy person who doesn't need specialised services with a long waitlist or a high price tag, it might be worth keeping the $60 a fortnight for yourself. Talk to a broker about your options – there may be a happy middle ground of cost versus benefit.

Same goes for life insurance. If you have kids and debts, like a mortgage, and you want to make sure these are taken care of if you die, then, yes, life insurance is very important for you to have. However, if you are a single guy chilling with your bros most nights, then let's just say that your money may be better spent elsewhere.

Contents insurance is similar again. If you don't own much, and it wouldn't matter if most of it was gone, then don't worry about contents insurance. But if you inherited a rare antique from old Aunt Jude then yeah, probably get that insured.

Are you getting the idea?

Now you know which insurances you need, how do you get a lower price on them?

One thing you can rely on is insurance companies trying to steal each other's customers. They always want the biggest market share possible. That's why they run promotions and offer discounts – free things! Yay! (Public service announcement: if they're selling you insurance out of a white van in a dark street, that is not an insurance company, my friend. Call 111.) We, the customers, can take advantage of these deals. When you first get insurance, shop around. Look at as many different places as you can to find the best deal at the time. Most insurance companies give free and quick quotes online.

You will need to choose an excess. This is the amount you will have to pay before the insurance company pays for a claim (or the amount that will be deducted from your payout). The higher the excess you opt for, the lower your regular payments will be. Be careful with this one. You can usually opt for a range from $200 to $2,000. Pick what you can afford. If you have savings or know that you could rustle up a higher amount of money if needed, then great, go for the higher excess. But if you know you won't be able to get much money together if the worst happens, pick a lower option. Then, once you are in the swing of managing your money and you have built up some savings, go back and raise your excess to save some of your hard-earned cash.

Keep on top of your insurance by checking your rates each year. Note down how much you are paying each week or fortnight, and get new quotes from other companies. It is normal for prices to go up over the years, particularly for something like life insurance, but it is still worth comparing rates. Sometimes you can even get a new quote from the company you are currently with to get a better rate – I have done this multiple times!

When comparing rates between companies, if you find that you'll save money by swapping, then go for it! It's easy to switch, and you can normally cancel old insurance policies online. Just make sure you have the new policy in place before you cancel the old one, and remember that with a new policy there may be a waiting period before you can make a claim (check the fine print).

Before we finish on insurance, here are a few more handy tips.

- If you don't already have car insurance, the best thing you can do is AT LEAST get third-party cover. Third-party means that if you rear-end a hotshot lawyer's $300,000 BMW, you won't be forced to pick up the bill for the damage to their car. Car insurance will save you from being in debt for the rest of your life, and it's one of the cheapest insurances.

- If you don't understand something when you're researching your options, ask. Google it or talk to someone who understands and can help you. There is nothing wrong with asking questions. There is everything wrong with getting the wrong insurance.

- Check in with your rates and get new quotes when big things happen. When you turn 25, car insurance companies won't class you as risky anymore and will give you a cheaper rate. When you get your full licence, the same rules apply. Same goes when you install an alarm system in your house – make sure you contact your insurance company to tell them, because they won't update your rate automatically. Remember, their goal is to make as big a profit as possible.

- As a rule of thumb, be wary of any insurance that the main companies don't offer. For example, mechanical insurance for if your car breaks down (this is different from roadside assistance, which is a useful thing to have). There is normally a very good reason that more reputable companies don't offer a particular insurance, and it can be a red flag if someone is trying to sell it to you. Google customer reviews for the provider, and you'll probably find a lot of negative reviews saying the company didn't pay up when they were supposed to. And yes, I'm speaking from experience ...

Utilities

Utilities are services like power, water, rubbish removal and internet. As with insurance costs, you shouldn't pay more for utilities than you need to – it's not like you'll get fancy electricity because you pay more. Nine times out of ten, you will be paying for EXACTLY the same service, just with a different logo and a different person on the phone line if something goes wrong.

So shop around. Get the best deals, and make sure you check in often to compare rates. Think outside the box: do you need an old-school internet plan if your phone provider offers a data plan that makes more financial sense? Look at all your options, and figure out the cheapest one that works for you.

Try to stay away from plans that offer something 'free' – like a TV if you sign up for 24 months. The company is often charging you for the 'free' appliance in the pricing plan. Nothing comes free, my friends.

And yes, once again, I've been there and got sucked into that. I did get a nice TV though.

Subscriptions

Subscriptions include Netflix, Spotify and all your other pay-by-the-month services. I'm not against these, but I'd recommend that you try to cut them down. Cancel any you are not using – subscriptions can seem cheap individually, but they add up quickly when you have more than a few accounts. The last time I calculated mine I thought the total would come to about $40 per month. It was sitting at $160. Whoops.

Food

At the time of writing, New Zealand is facing a record-high cost of living, which is having a severe impact on how expensive food is at the moment. A few years ago my family of four would spend around $120 to $140 a week on groceries. Now it's anywhere from $200 to $240 a week, and it could very easily be more. We are vegetarians, so we are lucky not to be affected by the price of meat, but I know that's gone sky high too!

How do we reduce our food bill? We try as many different things as possible. Gone are the days when one supermarket had all the cheaper items. We shop around for the best price. The bulk of our food comes from Pak'nSave, while the rest comes from Countdown. We also visit other supermarkets, like New World, sometimes. The Grocer app is great for comparing prices by supermarket. We tend not to go through every item, as we have found Pak'nSave to be cheaper overall, but we keep an eye on the bigger-cost items, like cat food (which can vary in price by up to $8 between stores!). We also get some of our fruit and vegetables from a co-op down the road, which gathers produce from local farms and bundles it together. We pay $15 a week, and the produce is always super fresh (mostly harvested the same day) and great quality. In a supermarket, the same bundle would normally cost us around $45. Why not see if you have a co-op local to you?

We also try (we are learning!) to grow our own produce. We have planted fruit trees and made veggie gardens. This is a great way to cut down on costs (once your garden is established) and it's also good for your mental health – gardening is a great way to practise mindfulness. If you have neighbours who grown their own food too, you could ask if they'd like to swap produce with you.

Transport

If you, like me, have eyes, you will have seen the crazy price of petrol. In high school I owned a tiny two-door diesel Peugeot. It used to cost $40 to fill the tank of this little beauty, and it would last two weeks! That was only back in 2016, so pretty decent going. Funnily enough I just searched online for that car and I found one for sale … for $12,000. Maybe I should have kept it as an investment – I only bought it for a few hundred!

Nowadays my household has two cars. Kaitlyn drives a fancier car with all the bells and whistles that costs on average $140 to fill, and a full tank would not last two weeks! Our other car is an oldie that I use to get to the train station and back for work. I have been tempted many times to sell it and buy something nicer, but I'm glad I haven't. For one, it's not a necessary expense. For two, I have other, far more pressing things to pay for!

There is a lot of pressure to try to keep up with the Joneses in modern life, and cars have become – or maybe they always have been – status symbols we can brag about without trying. I mean, we all have to get from A to B regardless, and getting there in a flashy car just happens to be the way some of us do it. Unless people are coming round to your place for dinner, they're not going to know if you have a big fridge or a marble benchtop, but everyone can see what car you drive.

Nice cars are also more affordable than flash houses, so people tend to spend money on the nice car first. The problem with this is that they are buying the lifestyle first, which will not help them get ahead financially. I am all for buying yourself a nice car – Kaitlyn and I just did – but only after you've progressed significantly with financial goals that will help your income and wealth grow, not just your image.

If you are looking to buy a new car, consider an electric car. You might think an EV is far more expensive but hear me out – it's worth thinking about the cost over a long period of time, not just upfront.

Let's break it down. At the time of writing, the cheapest electric car to buy brand new is an MG, which will cost you around $42,000 after the clean-car rebate. It has a seven-year warranty, so let's say you own it for that long. If you fill up your car with petrol once a week, the equivalent would be fully charging your MG about twice a week. Over seven years, that will cost you about $6,188 in electricity using today's rate. If you were to then sell the car, an online estimator says you would get about $18,000 for it. Overall you will have spent around $30,000 over seven years to drive a nice SUV with all the latest tech.

Let's compare that to one of the cheapest petrol cars on the market, a Suzuki Swift. One of these, brand new, would set you back around $20,000 after the clean-car rebate. Not bad, right? But now let's factor in petrol. Over seven years, at today's rate, petrol would cost you around $31,000! More than you paid for the car! Then let's say you sell it. According to the same online sales estimator, you might get around $10,000 for it. That's $40,000 spent in seven years! And that's without the extra mod cons and space the MG would give you. (I didn't include maintenance in the figures for either option as the cost would be relatively similar – although there is less to maintain on an electric car!)

Okay, this might all sound a bit biased, and it is. I love the look of that MG. But the numbers also speak for themselves. If you're considering what to spend on a vehicle, look at the cost of owning it over however long you intend to own it.

I'll also say this: buying a brand-new car is not the smartest thing to do. The amount brand-new cars depreciate in the first few years is massive! If you want something that feels new, get a car that's a few years old, in good nick and has already gone through the majority of its super-fast depreciation. (Most cars will continue to depreciate quite a bit, but not as fast as they do in the first few years.)

That's what Kaitlyn and I did with our new car. We bought it when it was just four years old and still under warranty. It had sold brand new for $55,000, and we got it for $20,000 less. Sucks for the first guy, but great for us!

Obviously cars are not the only form of transport. Catch public transport if you can – it will help to reduce your travel costs a lot. If that's not possible, look into carpooling to help share the cost with people who work and live near you. There are a few websites out there that can link you with people who live in your area and travel to the same area for work. Alternatively, if you live close enough to where you need to get to, you could walk or bike. I personally love biking and wish I lived closer to work to be able to bike. There are some really great community bike groups that can also help you to maintain or repair your bike if needed, helping to keep you active and save money at the same time!

Free stuff

Finally, don't underestimate the most obvious way to cut down your expenses: find free things to do instead of spending money!

free ways to get an instant mood boost

Put clean sheets on your bed

Have a home dance party

Get outside in nature

Make a plan you'll look forward to

Stay off social media for 24 hours

Make a hot drink in your favourite mug

Cuddle a pet

Exercise

Call a friend

free summer family activities

Bike rides

Local walks

Blow bubbles

Scavenger hunt

Obstacle course

DIY sensory bin

Library visit

Make ice blocks

Swim at your local beach or river

Camp on the trampoline

DIY marble run

Build a cardboard box fort

Chapter 3

Debt

Well, well. Now we are on to the big one. Debt. The one with the pointy teeth. Debt can help you achieve your goals, like buying a house, but it can also be the rock on your back that can break you if it's not managed properly. The way I think about debt is to see it as a business. Any debt that you incur is someone's business. For example, banks make a profit off your mortgage and your credit card. Debt inevitably incurs fees or interest, as this is how banks and other lenders make money. Any debt includes the actual cost of the item as well as the fees or interest on top.

There is good debt and there is bad debt. Good debt is debt that you must get to pay for an important thing, like a house or an education – something likely to improve your long-term situation. An asset.

Bad debt is everything else. It's debt for things that you don't need, and it racks up over time. For example, a particularly wild ASOS splurge with Afterpay. Bad debt can also occur when you use that debt for small essential purchases that lead into a bit of a debt spiral.

A lot of people ask me why I am so against buy now, pay later schemes when they don't charge interest. 'Isn't this good debt?' they ask.

My answer? No.

Again, think of it as a business. Buy now, pay later schemes are not there to help you afford things in an easier way; they are there to make a profit off you. They often have no interest … until you don't meet the payments. They are banking on you not making those payments, and they will win more than you do.

Buy now, pay later schemes are not there to help you afford things in an easier way; they are there to make a profit off you.

Sadly, the reality in New Zealand right now is that people have fallen into the buy now, pay later trap. Hear me when I say this: it is hands-down a trap. If someone feels like they can't afford something upfront, or they would rather pay for it over time to avoid the pain of paying (see Chapter 5), and they use one of these services, they fall into the trap. On their next payday, when they have to pay the next instalment, they often borrow again to be able to afford the next thing. Here is a visual of what this looks like.

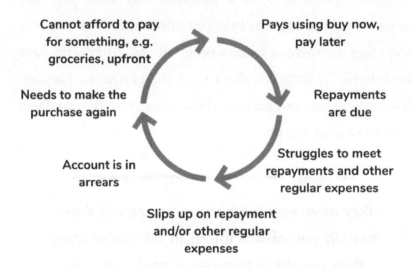

how buy now, pay later can trap those on low incomes in a cycle of debt

Cannot afford to pay for something, e.g. groceries, upfront

Pays using buy now, pay later

Needs to make the purchase again

Repayments are due

Account is in arrears

Struggles to meet repayments and other regular expenses

Slips up on repayment and/or other regular expenses

It's a spiral, and it's easy to get stuck in it. The best thing to do? Don't ever buy something through one of these services. If you can't afford something now, you certainly won't be able to afford it when you have to pay a debt on top of it! And, if you can afford it, pay for it with cash – you might even be able to get a cheaper price this way! Don't fall into temptation and end up spending more than you would have otherwise. It might not be as gratifying to delay a purchase and save up for it, but you will save so much more than dollars by doing it this way.

These services are particularly nasty. They would trap anyone and everyone if they could. They don't check your credit. They don't care if you can't afford to pay it back. In fact, they rely on you not being able to afford to pay it back. Then they can charge you a huge interest rate on what you owe. Not so much easy fun then!

alternatives to buy now, pay later

Get free financial advice, e.g. MoneyTalks

Ask if old-school layby is an option

Look into bartering in your community

Community initiatives, e.g. food banks, pātaka kai

Set up a sinking fund for upcoming costs

Set up an emergency fund for future unknowns

Look into small, safe, interest-free loans, e.g. Good Shepherd or Ngā Tāngata Microfinance

Could you choose a cheaper option and pay with cash?

Explore cheaper alternatives, e.g. secondhand, homemade or different brands

A scary cousin of buy now, pay later services are wage-advance services. Essentially these are just like buy now, pay later, but they provide you with your 'wage' before you are due to be paid. You have to pay interest on the loan, and when your employer pays you, you are due to repay the lender. You can imagine the problem: instead of using buy now, pay later for a specific purchase, you are borrowing your wage before it comes in to pay for multiple things. You are then charged interest and must pay it back quickly. This means that when your wage does come in, you are paying back a loan for the very thing you needed. But now you have even less and will need to borrow again. This spiral is also frighteningly fast to fall into – very soon you could end up owing your full wage or more, leaving you with no options and no ability to pay the loans back.

These services do not care about you at all. Their marketing, messaging and customer service might make it seem like they do, like they just want to help, but they are here for one thing only: to make money. One of these providers once threatened legal action over a $100 loan … to a homeless person.

predatory lending

Wage-advance services are particularly marketed towards people on low incomes, those struggling with impulse spending, and those with shopping addictions.

This is because these people make them the most money.

Most of these services charge a 'flat fee' of 5% on the loan, which you have to pay each time you take out a loan. This might not seem like a lot, but let's do the maths. If someone takes out a $100 wage-advance loan every fortnight for a year, and pays $5 each time, they will pay $130 in fees across the year – an interest rate of 130% p.a. No other credit provider can charge this crazy level of interest.

Debt can play a huge part in our lives. It can destroy self-confidence, happiness, relationships and so much more. Debt can come with a lot of stress, and it can also come with shame. There is a real taboo around debt – and not just about having it. People can feel shame about not having debt, too. Recently, I did a poll on my Instagram that had about 300 responses. I asked if people felt shame around debt and talking about it. Nearly all said yes. I followed up with: 'Do you feel more shame in having a large debt or small/no debt?' I was not expecting the response – it was split almost exactly 50/50.

I decided to look deeper into this result and messaged some of the people who'd responded. I found that those with large debts were ashamed because they felt like they were failing at life. On the other hand, those with little to no debt felt ashamed or embarrassed to talk about doing well when others were not. I'll talk more about this taboo in Chapter 5, but isn't it interesting? We all face debt at some point in our lives. We all have challenges to overcome.

I think the best way to approach it is to talk about it. Just think: if you have high debt and you talk about it, you may find many others in your position. You could free yourself from the burden of shame and empower others to do the same. For those with little to no debt, if you share your success and ways you achieved it, you may inspire others to lower their debt levels. All good things, my friends!

Clearly it's best to avoid debt where you can and to pay it off as fast as possible if you have it. But don't feel stink if you have debt. When I first started sorting my money out, I had about $5,000 in debt through several different places and I was living in overdraft. I also had no assets that I could sell to pay off my debt, and I had to work really hard to get myself out.

If you feel like you're in a situation where bad debt is unavoidable, talk to a financial advisor, your local Citizen's Advice Bureau or someone else who can help. There are services out there that offer no-interest loans for people in tight spots. Getting into a high-interest debt spiral is avoidable.

When I started the journey to get rid of my debt, I would use all my savings each week to pay off as much as possible. But I still found the debt overwhelming. It was loaned through lots of different places, so to make things easier on myself I decided to get a consolidation loan. A consolidation loan is when you take out a loan (yes, another loan – ironic, right?) with a bank and they pay off all your debts at once. Then you just make one regular payment to the bank to pay off the consolidation loan.

Getting a consolidation loan isn't a good idea for every person – it depends on your circumstances. If some of your debt is interest-free, getting a consolidation loan may not be the best approach because they often charge interest. But do what works for you. At the end of the day, you know yourself best – if having one loan to pay off will feel more achievable to you than having multiple, then go for it.

When you begin saving money and reducing your bills, wiping out all your debts should be your first goal. There are a few different tried-and-tested ways to focus on paying off your debts.

3 ways to pay off debt

avalance it

Pay the largest or highest-interest debt as quickly as you can.

Pay minimums on other debts.

PROS:
High-interest debt out of the day.

consolidate it

Combine all debts into one through bank or lender.

PROS:
Less overwhelming, easier to focus.

snowball it

Pay the smallest debt as quickly as you can.

Pay minimums on other debts.

PROS:
Quick wins = good confidence boost.

1. **The avalanche method** focuses on clearing the biggest debts first, like a car loan. By doing so, you will save a lot on interest. Make sure that you continue to pay minimum repayments on all other debts at the same time to avoid fees.

2. **The consolidation method** is the one I mentioned earlier. Taking out a consolidation loan can help you minimise high interest rates across a lot of different debts if you can consolidate with a lower rate. People often do this with their mortgage – they bring other debts into the mortgage to reduce the number of different payments they have to make, and the amount of interest they're paying. Some community providers do no-interest consolidation loans to support people who are struggling financially. Check them out to see if you might be eligible.

3. **The snowball method** focuses on smaller debts first, like overdrafts or credit card debt – it's basically the opposite of the avalanche method. Start with the smallest debt you have – maybe a parking fine? Pay it off, and then go to the next one. The more debts you pay off, the more of a sense of achievement you will feel, which will motivate you to keep going. While you are working your way through the list, make sure that

you keep paying all minimum repayments on other debts to avoid fees.

Set up a regular payment that you can afford and that won't be too tight, and then stick to it. Add lump sums to it if you get any extra money. Once you get rid of your debt, a whole world of possibilities will open up – you'll be able to do so much more with your savings! And, hey, if debt repayments are one of your regular bills, then look at you – you just got rid of a bill!

the debt-free journey

1 Believe in yourself

2 Set up an emergency fund

3 Commit to not adding to your debt

4 Reduce your expenses

5 Stick to a realistic budget

6 Choose an approach (e.g. avalanche, snowball or consolidation)

7 Keep showing up and make it happen!

Of course, there will be times when even these methods do not work. Sometimes, debt might get someone so far in a hole that even good budgeting methods won't be able to pull them out. This is when a lot of people start looking bankruptcy in the face. Bankruptcy is when someone declares to the government that they can no longer meet repayments on their debt. It's a last resort. It's the option you take when you have no other choice, because it can have serious implications.

There are three levels of insolvency in New Zealand: a Debt Repayment Order, if you owe under $50,000 and can repay some of the debt; a No Asset Procedure, if you owe under $50,000 and you can't repay any; and finally there's bankruptcy if you owe more than $50,000. Each has its own set of rules and consequences. (You can technically file for bankruptcy for debts of just $1,000, but this option is only really advised for those with debts of more than $50,000.)

If you declare bankruptcy, it will become near-impossible for you to borrow in the future, your career will have more limited options (some employers only want people who have never been bankrupt for certain roles), and you won't be able to be a director of a company for three years. Also, while you're under a bankruptcy order (which typically lasts three years), you'll have to get permission if you want to leave New Zealand, manage any part of a company, become self-employed or become employed by a relative's business. The information on your bankruptcy will become public, and your bankruptcy will affect your partner's and any joint finances. Essentially, you will cripple your financial standing.

That's why I say bankruptcy should be avoided at all costs, even though it sometimes seems unavoidable. Before declaring bankruptcy, try to negotiate with creditors on your payment terms, find other sources of cash to repay your debts (can you sell any assets?), seek professional advice, or see if something like a consolidation loan would work for you. There are also organisations that will support you to repay small debts with zero-interest loans, such as Ngā Tāngata Microfinance, a non-profit organisation backed by Kiwibank.

Financial advisors can help, and a good place to start finding one might be your local Citizen's Advice Bureau, or you can try community organisations or government departments. Just make sure any organisation you go to for 'help' is truly there to help you, not rope you into debt that is worse for you in the long term.

Let's talk about credit cards

To me, credit cards are not smart. They fall under the bad debt category. I have only ever had one in my life, and I maxed it out almost instantly. This was when I was super bad with money, and I'd spend anything I could get my hands on. So I get it: when you find some new way to spend or you suddenly have money or a new credit limit, you can feel on top of the world. It feels great to have this new spending power. But the feeling doesn't last. Once you've spent it all with a credit card, the high is gone. And it won't come back. Because you'll now need to work to pay all the money back. And chances are you won't. Chances are you will stay in the red, and your debt will fluctuate up and down without ever really being paid off.

One of the most worrisome problems of credit cards is that they can have an impact on your ability to get good debt if you need it. Merely having a credit card in your name can be enough for a bank to decline your mortgage application. Even if you have a credit card you never use, it can be held against you. According to Mortgage Lab, every $1,000 limit you have on a credit card equates to about $4,300 less that banks will lend you to buy a house. So is it worth it?

how credit cards can get you into trouble

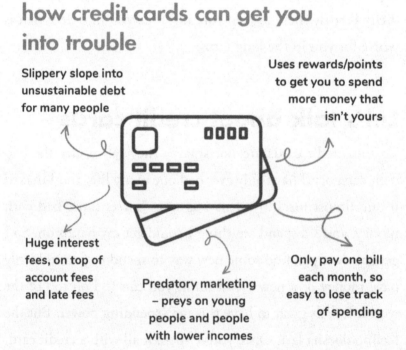

Slippery slope into unsustainable debt for many people

Uses rewards/points to get you to spend more money that isn't yours

Huge interest fees, on top of account fees and late fees

Predatory marketing – preys on young people and people with lower incomes

Only pay one bill each month, so easy to lose track of spending

Let me tell you a story. It's about me. Lucky you.

When I was 18, I had a decent-enough job and I was earning a decent-enough amount of money. However, I was in no way rich, and I had no proper assets to my name. For the most part, I seemed to be doing better than a lot of people my age. So I started spending. HARD.

It didn't take long for me to 'need' more money. So I got an overdraft. You know those student overdrafts that the bank says will be interest-free (until they aren't) and will give you free chips or some shit? Yeah, one of them.

Within weeks that line of credit was gone. All of it. And I was living in debt.

Did I do the smart thing and change the way I was living? Nope. No chance in hell. I just thought, 'I need more money.'

So I got another job. Now I was working about 60 hours a week. And I had money again! Which meant I could spend more! And I did!

And what happened? I didn't have enough money. I 'needed' more.

I got a credit card. And maxed it out.

I started putting things like $2,000 stereos on hire purchase. (You know the ads: ****BUY NOW, PAY LATER! 60 MONTHS INTEREST-FREE!****)

And then no one would lend me money anymore. I couldn't work more hours because I would collapse under the stress of it all. I got a pay rise, but again it wasn't enough.

The penny dropped, a bit too late for my liking: I couldn't earn my way out of my spending habits.

You shouldn't spend more as you begin to make more. Doing that will NEVER, EVER get you to your goals.

Did you know that most Lotto winners go broke? Most people who come into large sums of money and who already have spending problems will spend it all without even noticing. It's like an illness. And the first step is to admit you have a problem.

Okay, okay. This is getting a bit self-help-y and kind of Kumbaya-ish. Go do a shot of vodka or something and come back.

I know a lot of people will now be thinking, 'But credit cards are great! They give you rewards!'

Yes, that is true. But a credit card that gives you rewards, like Airpoints, is also likely to have an annual fee. These fees can be high. The interest is even higher.

'But they are worth it for the points! I will earn more points than the fee costs!'

Maybe. Often you'll earn points at a pretty shocking rate – something like $1 in Airpoints for every $100 spent. How much will you have to spend to earn enough Airpoints to break even? Will it tempt you to spend more than you usually would?

You will also pay fees on a lot of purchases. Retailers often charge you to use a credit card, which means you are paying more than me for the same thing. Stink.

'But I pay off my card every month so I don't get charged interest!'

Oh cool, good for you! Chances are that this won't always be the case. In fact, it's very likely it's not always the case. Why else would these cards exist? They know people won't make their payments sooner or later, and that's when they hit them with massively high interest rates.

Think about where those points are coming from. The credit card companies are not giving them to you out of the kindness of their hearts. They are paying for them with their revenue. Which they get when people can't pay off their credit cards. That gives me the ick.

I am yet to find something I need that can't be sorted with my debit card, using my own money, with no fees.

what's the deal with debit cards?

Looks like a credit card, but uses your own money

Can't get into debt – can only use what's in your account

Can usually block/unblock card via an app if lost of stolen

An easy way to limit spending if you struggle with impulse buying

Can be used for online shopping like a credit card

Money mistakes

I want to tell you about a few money mistakes that Kaitlyn and I have made and that I know other people have made. Why? Hopefully it will help you to avoid the same mistakes – or at least feel less alone if you have already made them too!

money mistakes we've made before

Living in overdraft

Getting locked in to an expensive contract with a power company because they gave a 'free' appliance on sign-up (see page 34)

Living beyond our means

Going with the 'cheapest' option for earthworks and losing thousands because of it

Quitting a job to find a new job (see page 67)

Buying things on finance

Jumping into tertiary education and student loans

1. Living beyond your means

If you spend more than you make, you are living beyond your means and will no doubt end up in debt. You could end up in a debt spiral, like using buy now, pay later schemes to stay afloat and only sinking further. Best thing to do?

Live like you are earning less. I get this may not always be possible, but if you start making more money and you don't desperately need that money to cover your living costs, make sure you are intentionally spending less than you earn. And no, not by one or two dollars (that doesn't count!) – try a percentage that works for you, like 5% or 10%.

reminder:

social media has normalised mindless, excessive spending.

most people don't regularly buy hauls of clothes. they just wear what they already have.

live your life according to what's within your means.

2. Living in overdraft

This is something Kaitlyn and I did when we were first together. We each had one of those student accounts with little to no interest that gave us an overdraft of a few thousand. Living in it was such an easy trap to fall into. It only took one or two big shops to plunge into it. We were on low wages, living paycheque to paycheque, and there was seemingly no way to climb out of the hole.

This happens to so many people. They get an overdraft, credit card or other line of credit, use it, and then find themselves unable to pay the debt back. Think before you act: will you be able to pay the money back?

3. Jumping into tertiary education

The act of becoming students and jumping into university straight after high school was a bad financial call – for both me and Kaitlyn! We were taught that going to university was one of our only options after high school, that there was no other real choice – unless we wanted to work at McDonald's for the rest of our lives. So we both jumped straight into degrees. As did almost everyone else we knew.

I quickly figured out that university wasn't for me and left after just one semester, although by that time I had racked up $5,000 in student loans. Kaitlyn left her degree after a year and a half to begin a new one from scratch that was more in line with her interests. She finished that degree and now has over $50,000 in student loans. Her current job has nothing to do with her degree.

My point is this: we racked up debt – albeit 'good debt' to further our education – without really understanding who we were and what we wanted to do with our lives. If we could go back, we would take a gap year to explore the world of work and understand what we did and didn't like. Then we would pursue degrees, IF they were needed for our lines of work. Both of us currently work in fields where having a degree is not necessary.

Don't get me wrong – going to university to get a degree is not a bad thing by any means. But doing it when you are unsure of your purpose and the end goal for the degree is just wasting money.

4. Going for the cheapest option

Okay, so it may sound like I am about to go against all my own advice here and tell you to start buying the most expensive things. Not quite. The motto 'buy something quality and it will last longer' is often true, but when it comes to things like utilities and everyday items I still recommend going for the cheapest option. However, I stress caution if you're doing something that involves a large amount of money being spent anyway, like renovations or building a house.

When Kaitlyn and I set out to build our house, we first had to retain the driveway so trucks could get down to the section. We received multiple quotes, ranging from $18,000 to $65,000 (for three retaining walls, including the driveway). Naturally, we went with the cheapest option.

In hindsight, alarm bells should have been ringing. The other two quotes were similar – both in the range of $65,000 – but we were happy we could get the job done for a much lower cost. The contractor we hired gave us all the reassurances, telling us he had been doing jobs like this

his whole life (which was true). Unfortunately, for whatever reason, he decided to do our job extremely slowly and extremely badly. He never applied for council consent and he never consulted an engineer – as a result he built the retaining wall wrong, even using the wrong materials (fence posts!).

When our builder came along to inspect the site for the house, he immediately noticed that the retaining wall was not to code. It wouldn't hold a car, let alone a concrete truck!

After a long back-and-forth with the contractor, we ended up getting $5,000 back. But, between the money we'd already spent and the increase in costs over the *SIX MONTHS* we were dealing with this situation, we lost around $80,000.

We had to start all over again and ended up paying roughly $65,000, the same amount we could have spent at the start, on top of losing 80k.

Lesson. Learnt.

5. Buying things on finance

By now, you will have no doubt as to how I feel about buying things on finance: just don't do it. Save up to buy something – set a good habit! Show yourself you can work *for* an item, not work *off* an item. As a little example, let's look at a car loan.

Interest fees on car loans vary A LOT. You could get a loan from around 6% to 20% or more, depending on the provider, your credit rating and other factors. Let's say you want to buy a car for $15,000. You agree to a big bank rate of 13.9% p.a. Car loans are typically for five to seven years. Say you choose five years. You have a monthly repayment of $351, and you will end up paying $5,933.70 in interest alone – over one third of what you are borrowing! Your total bill, including loan establishment fees, will be $21,032.70. On a car. And the entire time you are paying it off, it will be depreciating in value – by the time it's paid off, it might be worth half that if you are lucky.

Save for things, my friends. And if you urgently need a car and you have to borrow money to get it, buy something that meets your needs for as little as possible. A car is a liability and not worth going broke over. Let the status symbol go.

Debt marketing

It's easy to understand why so many of us make these mistakes and end up in debt: we humans have got really good at marketing debt to ourselves. Debt isn't sold as something that stays with you for a long time, clinging to the back of your throat like a phlegmy cold that just won't leave, costing you loads more than you bargained for. Ew. And why would it be? Who would want that?

No, debt is marketed as a way to achieve your glamorous dreams – now. It's all about instant gratification. Go on that wonderful holiday! Get that car! Man, you NEED those sunnies. And getting them is just so easy! Don't worry, we got you. Don't think about your debt – think about your shiny new thingy! Woo! They want you to believe that you will be instantly gratified, and that it's the easiest thing to get there.

Just like that, we are hooked. But the high, the excitement, will be gone as soon as the novelty wears off. And you will be left with debt. You'll have to slog to pay it off. All the glamour will be gone and in its place you'll have stress – and shame.

I wonder what it would look like if we made debt retailers put warnings on their products or ads like those on cigarettes, alcohol and gambling. Would they use a picture of someone crying over their bills? A slogan, perhaps: 'Borrow responsibly'. Or maybe they'd set up a self-help phone line? This might all sound a bit funny, but really I think it is necessary. People are not warned about the very real risks that come with debt. There are so many ploys not only to make debt seem like the best option, but the obvious choice! Have you ever paused and thought, 'But why do I *need* to put this on a credit card?'

I want you to take a second look at debt – maybe if enough of us do, it will create a change in our behaviour. We might rethink this hyped-up obsession we all have. I get messages every week from people who have paid off credit cards, personal loans and all sorts of other debts, and every time I am so happy for them.

If you know that you can sometimes be sucked in by debt marketing, try to think ahead. What ways might you avoid it? Follow accounts on social media that post content that encourages you to avoid or get out of debt, and those that share great tips and tricks to help. All these actions add up, and they might help you avoid more debt-ridden mistakes!

Chapter 4

Increase your income

Here's where the fun begins!

It's time to earn like you've never earned before ... but how do you earn more? How do you grow your income to reach your goals?

Well, I will start by reminding you that no matter what your income is, earning more is not the only way to get ahead. Increasing your earnings may be great for your bank balance, but your work needs to be sustainable and not something that will burn you out. That's why I talked about how to cut down your spending first, before talking about ways to earn more money.

With that caveat out of the way, let's get into some of the ways you can boost your earnings.

You and your job

Get a new job

Wow, ground-breaking stuff, right? Not really, but I want to talk about how to get a new job that will raise your income. First rule: never leave a job to find a job. That is career sabotage, and your bank balance will not thank you. Start looking for a new job while you are in your current role. If you don't know where to begin or what kind of job to look for, try out a role-finder or strength-based quiz. You can normally find these online for free, and they suggest roles you might like based on your answers. CareerQuest on careers.govt.nz is a good place to start. Otherwise, talk to family and friends and get their ideas. They might be able to provide some insight on what you're good at.

If you're looking for a new job, make sure it will pay you more and that you like the sound of it. It doesn't have to be something you have done before, but something that matches your skills, strengths or experience is the priority.

In an interview, you're likely to be asked how much you'd like to be paid, so always do your research first. You need to know how much other people are paid in the same or similar roles in other organisations, so you have a rough figure on what to expect. Consider how much experience other people in these roles have in relation to how much they are being paid. Pro tip: people hired as contractors (meaning they don't have a permanent contract) are usually paid a much higher rate, but contracting doesn't offer stability so it's not the right option for everyone.

Let your potential employer say the first number. You never know, they might have a higher number in mind and you don't want to shoot yourself in the foot! Then, once they've named their figure, consider asking for more – even if it was more than you expected. There is an art to this. Be polite and thank them sincerely for the offer. Talk about your goals and the reality of how much you 'need' to earn. Make it about your cost of living and your aspirations, not about greed. Offer a counter figure. If they've offered you a bit more than you were expecting, go up slightly but not too much. If they've offered you less, go up higher than you usually would. Chances are they will meet you somewhere in the middle. If they offer you way more than you had hoped, well, take that and run!

Keep in mind that all of this assumes the employer has the wiggle room to be able to offer you more. If they can't, and if the number they offered is not enough, politely decline. You are perfectly within your rights to turn down a job that is not the right fit for you. It's a big decision, and not one to rush into because you feel like you have to take the first thing you're offered.

Ask for a pay rise

If you are already in a role and doing well, you are probably more likely than you realise to get a pay rise. Most workplaces won't give you a pay rise unless you ask for one. There are exceptions to this – some workplaces give automatic raises each year to keep up with inflation – but most of the time, and even if your workplace is one of the exceptions, it is a good idea to ask. If you don't ask, you don't get!

When planning to ask for a pay rise, write down all the reasons you would like one. Consider the following:

1. What have been some of your big achievements in the role?
2. How have you grown or developed?
3. What have you done well?
4. Have you done any training lately?
5. Have you taken on more responsibility?
6. Do you do things that are outside your role?
7. Have you been in the workplace a long time?

Write down answers to all these, and centre your request on them.

Next, set up a meeting with your manager and be upfront. In the meeting, mention that you are requesting a pay rise and list all your reasons. Make sure you talk about your goals and what the extra money would be used for. This will make you seem more driven and less greedy. (Not that it is greedy to ask to be paid more, but a good impression helps.) Offer your manager the opportunity to go away and think about it – especially if you get the feeling that they might say no on the spot!

Have a figure in mind. If all goes well, get them to present you with an offer first, and then follow the same tactics described above to negotiate pay in a new job.

If your manager declines to give you a pay rise, ask when they will be able to consider one and under what circumstances. This will help you understand what you need to do to earn a pay rise.

Be the squeaky wheel. Just because you have asked for a pay rise in the past does not mean you can't ask for one in the future. Obviously don't ask every week, but maybe every six months if you aren't getting any luck. If nothing seems to be working, it may be time to consider another job. Or else you might want to …

Ask for a promotion

A promotion normally always involves more pay. If you're struggling to get that pay rise in your current job, a promotion to a higher position could be the smart way to go about it. But how do you get one? Well, you waltz into your boss's office and demand one of course!

Kidding! Promotions often come, or so it seems in the movies, when your manager sees you doing a really great job and they want to reward you for it. This can happen – it has never happened to me, but I do know it's a thing. So that's the first step in getting a promotion: work hard. Promotions and pay rises don't just get handed out. You need to show that you are worth it and excelling in your role.

A good way to improve your chances of promotion is to find ways to upskill. If your work offers free courses or will support you to study and get additional qualifications, this could be a great way to show you are dedicated to being a valuable employee. New skills, hard work and good performance in your current role will all show your manager that you're ready for more.

Managers are not always actively looking for people to promote. Sometimes your workplace may publicly advertise a higher position so that anyone can apply. If this happens, you may also need to apply for it like you would any other role. It might feel a bit strange, but this will show your manager you want more. If you get an interview for the role, mention all the upskilling you have done and the experience you have gained since entering your current role.

If you want to beat the queue and get your name in the hat *before* a job is advertised, chat with your manager. I was working in a customer service role, and I knew that a manager position was coming up because the owners had been talking about it for a while. I wrote up a proposal outlining why I wanted to be the manager and all the ideas I had to improve the business. The owners were impressed with the thought and effort I had put in, and they offered me the promotion. You could try something similar if you have a chance to get in early.

If climbing higher in your workplace is something that's important to you, it's always a good idea to tell your manager. A supportive manager will help you get there and give you the guidance, advice and opportunities to succeed. And, as a bonus, you get to practise being more open and upfront! That way, you'll have no need to second-guess yourself, and you won't be merely hoping the manager knows you want a promotion.

Consider contracting

All the options I have talked about so far are all well and good if you are after, or want to stay in, a traditional job. I classify a traditional job as one where you sign an employment agreement and you are considered a permanent member of staff – so I'd include fixed-term roles, which are increasingly common.

But what if you want something else? Is there such a thing? Could you earn more doing the same job but with a different arrangement? Potentially, yes!

Contracting is a type of employment with very loose terms of engagement. There's often no notice period, sick leave, annual leave or guaranteed hours, but contracting can have higher rates of pay. For example, if I was working as a business analyst on a permanent contract, I might earn between $70,000–$80,000 per year. Not a bad wage! However, if I was to work as a contractor and pick up the right contract, I could earn around $120 per hour. Full-time that works out to be $201,600 per year. Pretty incredible!

But don't get too excited. While this might sound very tempting, there are drawbacks to contracting. First, not all professions offer this kind of money – you have to find the right role. Second, as well as the lack of job security and benefits already mentioned, contractors are likely to be contracted for short stints, say three months at a time.

Contracting is an option though, and I know plenty of people who do it – it's more common than you would think! If I didn't have family commitments, I would probably give it a whirl.

Contractors are considered sole traders (small businesses in their own right), and their tax is not done for them. If you work as a contractor, your remuneration will be paid directly into your bank account and you will have to deduct and pay your own tax as well as things like student loan payments and KiwiSaver contributions. It can be very easy to miscalculate your tax, especially if you are contracting for odd periods of time with differing rates. There are some pretty useful services out there that can do all this for you, and they are worth the money! Most don't cost too much and will potentially save you from over- or underpaying taxes.

You can also use these services to claim your costs as business expenses – and as a sole trader, there's a lot more you can claim on that you can't really do when you are earning as a 'regular' employee. Sole traders can claim a percentage of all their business-related costs, which are costs that they incur to earn money. These could include your phone, internet and travel costs, and even a portion of your rent or mortgage if you work from home. Claiming these as expenses can often result in a good tax refund from provisional tax paid at the end of the financial year.

Side hustles

I have had my fair share of side hustles over the years – probably more than my fair share, come to think of it. But I'm sure you're wondering what a side hustle is. I'm so glad you asked, dear reader! A side hustle is something you do on top of your day job, or your main income. A side hustle brings in some extra coin, and most of the time it's something you find fun and interesting. It's also best if it's relatively easy to begin making a profit from it. Not all side hustles fit this category though – I mean, I started a bakery. But more on that later.

To figure out what your side hustle could be, identify what you already do or like to do, and think about how you might make money from that.

To figure out what your side hustle could be, identify what you already do or like to do, and think about how you might make money from that.

A side hustle could also be another job, rather than something you do off your own back like running your own business. When I first left home and moved up to Auckland, I got myself multiple jobs. My customer service job was my main source of income, but I also did accounting and admin for a travel agency, relief work at a day care, product advising for Microsoft, and some mystery shopping – all in the space of one year.

Side hustles could even be something in between: part owning a business, part having another job. A year or two after moving to Auckland, when Kaitlyn and I were newly married, we decided to save for a house. We knew that if we wanted to buy in a short timeframe, we would need extra income. Being the impatient couple we are, we decided to start some side hustles. We joined up with a friend (so no one had to pay much upfront) to buy a car, and then we signed up to a company that allowed us to rent out our private vehicle to members of the public at a rate that we chose. The company was quite good, but they did take 40% off for insurances and their running costs. Eventually someone wanted to rent the car long-term, so we set up our own agreement and insurance to cut out the middleman. All in all, Kaitlyn and I made $7,000 in a year. (It would have been more, but the person renting the car crashed it halfway through the year and it took several weeks to repair. Sometimes you win and sometimes you learn!)

We also decided to do Uber Eats. We owned another car that we could use for deliveries, and we happened to live in a heavily populated area, which meant lots of potential orders. Uber Eats was pretty easy to start with. We would put in a few hours after work and university to make the most of the dinner rush. After a few months we stopped because it was taking a toll on our happiness and marriage (the bickering while driving was endless!). It still made us enough extra money that, put together with the $7,000 we earned from renting our car and our other savings, we were able to afford the deposit on the house we bought at the end of the year.

Not long after we bought our house, Kaitlyn and I befriended a young woman called Ellie whose baby was just a few weeks older than ours. We had the same midwife, and we happened to live just a few doors down from each other.

At her daughter's first birthday, we saw the most magnificent cake ever. It was stunning and I instantly asked where she'd bought it from. 'I didn't buy it,' she replied. 'I made it myself!'

My mouth dropped open. It was one of those cakes you see on Instagram. A real showstopper. And then I ate some and it was even more glorious – it tasted divine. And it was so moist (moist ☺)!

I'd thought my jaw couldn't drop any lower, but then Ellie said it was gluten-free. I had never in my life wanted to take another bite of something gluten-free, let alone another slice! But this was a cake dreams are made from.

Kaitlyn and I implored Ellie to sell her cakes. She said no, she couldn't. For the next 18 months, we kept half asking, half begging her to sell them. Until one day we came up with a plan. Kaitlyn and I would help Ellie sell her cakes – we'd do what we are good at, the business side, and Ellie could do what she's good at, the baking. Just like that we came together to create Ellie's new side hustle.

Starting a proper business as your side hustle is no easy task – it requires dedication and a LOT of time. There are so many hurdles and things to do when you're starting out. If you're considering it, the best thing to do right now is google 'starting a business' and have a look at the resources the New Zealand Government has put out on the subject. It's all very helpful! You may even be able to get some start-up funding.

After Ellie's business was up and running, I stumbled into a niche market I didn't even know existed. I had started buying decanters (old-school ones, often crystal, used for serving alcohol) and accidentally ended up with more than my wife deemed 'necessary'. Okay, the words she used were a bit more colourful than that, but you get the point. I had a lot. I went to sell some and discovered that they can sometimes go for a lot online. I decided to have some fun and market them as much as I could with a whole lot of pizzazz – something in which Kaitlyn was pivotal, being the amazing copywriter she is. I sold decanters at prices anywhere from $50 to $300, having only paid a fraction of that to acquire them. I ended up selling a lot over a short period of time and built up quite a following. Embarrassingly, people started coming up to me in the street to ask if I was that 'decanter guy'.

My decanter side hustle only went on for a short time as I soon moved my attention to writing my own books. You might have noticed I get bored easily!

Those are some of my side hustles, but what makes your juices start to flow? Can you find something that works for you? Here are some ideas for side hustles that are relatively easy to start and don't require too much prior knowledge.

1. Furniture flipping

Go to your local op-shop, Trade Me or Facebook Marketplace – anywhere that will have cheap secondhand furniture. Find something that looks dated and needs a bit of TLC – these pieces are often free or sold at very reasonable prices. Make sure the item is made fairly solidly. You don't want to work on something made from flimsy wood, particle board or substitute materials. Get a good old piece that you can make look new again. With natural wood items, you could sand down the blemishes (use sandpaper with a medium to fine grit) and apply a new stain or protective layer. Natural wood is also easy to paint (do light layers, and then give it a very light sand to finish). Check out how-to guides on YouTube or just freeball it and teach yourself – it's pretty easy.

how to make money upcycling furniture

Find free or cheap furniture online or at a recycling centre

Clean, do any necessary repairs and make a plan

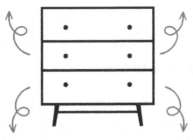

Sand, prime, paint and decorate, depending on the piece

Sell online and use a portion of the profit for the next piece

Once the item's cleaned up, sell it on for a profit!

Top tip: check for borers (bugs that make small holes in untreated wood), which could have hollowed out some pieces. The wood can be treated if the damage is minor, but if it is infested – steer clear!

2. Freelancing

If you are skilled at writing, editing, social media, website development, graphic design, or really anything that someone can ask you to do remotely, you could do some freelance work. (You could do things like videoing or photography if you are close by too!) Freelance work is typically one-off and needed in a short timeframe. There are a lot of websites out there where you can list your services and people will ask you to do work for them. It is a fairly crowded market, so aim for quality over quantity to build up loyal customers who know and like your style of work.

3. Green-thumb work

There are lots of lawns to mow, gardens to weed and trees to trim out there. Work your way around the neighbourhood and offer to do it for people. If you don't have all the tools and you need to borrow the client's, you could offer a lower rate.

If you get into this kind of work, ask to take cuttings of a plant (or a tree!) or two that you think you could grow. You could then use these cuttings to grow new plants to sell. You could even try growing fruit and veggies from cuttings or seeds from produce you buy at the supermarket.

4. Renting things out

Do you have specialty tools or equipment that other people might like to use? Spare space you're not using? A car parked in the garage gathering dust? Put these items to work and rent them out! There are websites where you can list different items to rent out locally, you could set up your own online store, or you could advertise in your neighbourhood. Remember to make sure you have insurance sussed before doing this.

5. Tutoring

Teach someone a skill you love! Do you know how to play an instrument? How to make a clay pot? Heck, how to make killer brownies? Teach someone! You'd be surprised how many people would love to learn something new – they might just never have got around to starting. Put the word out, and I'm sure a few people will take you up on the offer.

There is also classic tutoring if you can find students who are looking to master a skill or subject that you know a lot about.

6. House- and pet-sitting

When some people go on holiday or an extended trip, they like to have someone come and pet-sit or house-sit while they're away. There are really great websites you can sign up to (some cost money to join, but these are the best ones!) and use to create a profile, describing who you are and what sort of sitting you are looking to do. I know a lot of people who regularly pet-sit at people's houses – sometimes for months at a time.

House- and pet-sitting is often done for free, as the sitter receives free accommodation and utilities in exchange, but sometimes it is paid. If you are very well recommended and carry out extra duties (above and beyond feeding and walking animals) you can charge from $50 to $100 a day. It's a great way to earn money or save big on costs if you are flexible about where you live and how long for. Kaitlyn and I did this while we were building our new house. It was a lot of fun!

I hope these examples have helped inspire some ideas for your side-hustle journey. And, hey, you don't need to know exactly what you want to do right now. If you take anything away, I hope it is this: keep your eyes open for opportunities. They are everywhere when you look for them. Someone's lawn is always overgrown? Offer to mow it each week. Got a way with words? Offer to proofread and edit documents or websites. A whiz with computers? Find some freelance work online.

Please keep in mind that if you have too much on or you're already stressed as it is, having a side hustle might not be right for you at the moment. There's no point diving into something new if you don't have the energy or mental capacity for it. Jot down some ideas and come back to them later.

If you have a lot of side hustles and you're earning a consistent amount from them, then you will probably need to pay tax on these earnings. Filing your own taxes and figuring out how much you need to pay and what you can claim can be very confusing. Look into using a tax agent, who can file these things for you. They're worth the money!

A NOTE ON TAX

If you're an employee in a business, a sole trader or someone doing contract work, you will pay tax at your normal individual tax rate. At the time of writing, the current way this works in New Zealand is the first $14,000 an individual earns will be taxed at 10.5%. Each dollar after that up to $48,000 will be taxed at 17.5%. Each dollar after that up to $70,000 will be taxed at 30%, each dollar after *that* up to $180,000 at 33% and all remaining income over that amount will be taxed at 39%.

Say you are earning $75,000 a year of taxable income on tax code 'M' (main tax code without a student loan). You will pay:

- 10.5% on $14,000
- 17.5% on $34,000
- 30% on $22,000
- 33% on $5,000

So your total tax bill will be $15,670 before the ACC levy.

This might seem fair, it might not, but these are the current tax rates for individuals in New Zealand in 2023. Tax rates and thresholds change over time depending on government policy and, in New Zealand, may be about to change because of the recent change of government. But this will hopefully give you an idea on how it's split up.

Taxes are collected to pay for running the country. The government collects tax to run its departments, which distribute and legislate how the money is used and the way the country is governed. Taxes pay for everything you get as a citizen. For example, tax pays for benefits for people who have no or low income. It pays for social housing, law and order, major roading, education, health services, public infrastructure, initiatives and programmes to solve nationwide issues, and more. In short, your taxes pay for the country to operate and support all of its citizens.

Even though taxes are designed to support the many, there are people who pay less than their fair share. Rightly or wrongly, people can manage their money in ways that mean they pay less tax. One very common way is using a business to channel income. The flat tax rate for businesses is currently 28%, which means they won't be taxed at the same rate as individuals, who currently have a top tax rate of 39% – a difference of 11%. Businesses can also claim expenses on their income; for example, if a business claims a $4 expense on their $10 income, they will only pay tax on $6. Businesses work out as many ways as possible to legally claim expenses to reduce the amount of income they report and pay tax on. Businesses can also reinvest any profits in the business and end up paying no tax for the financial year. This is how someone earning even $40,000 a year could pay more in tax than a business making millions. This is all legal and it happens all the time, whether you agree with it or not.

Let your money work for you – invest!

Now things are starting to get really interesting. This is where I talk about getting your money to do the work while you sit back and relax! Have you ever heard the phrase 'work harder not smarter'? Don't be fooled – this is not a get-rich-quick scheme. You'll need to have some money to get you going. Not a big amount, but something in your back pocket.

Investing is what you want to do to advance your long-term position or goals. It's not a quick win – it requires patience and a plan. Investing is a way to build up your assets, which are things that will likely rise in value with time and could earn you real-time income. Liabilities are the opposite. A liability is anything that will decrease in value, or it can be money that you owe – something that you are financially responsible for that is likely not going to pay you back. (Kids don't count, guys. I mean, technically, yes, they are liabilities, but they are worth it ...)

I like thinking about assets and liabilities in this way: don't buy a lifestyle – buy an income. In other words, don't buy all the fancy cars, watches and so on. Buy something that will pay you back. What you do with the money you earn from your asset is up to you. But at least your asset will keep giving. A car won't.

— **"**—————————

I like thinking about assets and liabilities in this way: don't buy a lifestyle – buy an income. In other words, don't buy all the fancy cars, watches and so on. Buy something that will pay you back.

————————— **"** —

Shares

Letting your money work for you means setting up your money so it makes its own money. There are long-term and short-term investments, and they come in many different shapes and sizes. Let's start by talking about shares.

Shares are something you can invest in to own a part – a 'share' – of a company. Nearly every big business you can think of has shares for sale. Businesses often sell shares to raise money for the business. Say a business sells 1,000 shares to the public, and in total those shares are worth 10% of the business. If you buy 100 of these shares, you will own 1% of the business, and would be entitled to 1% of the business's profits at the end of the financial year. A financial year in New Zealand runs from 1 April to 31 March. When you receive this profit, it is called a dividend. You must pay tax on dividends because they count as income.

Often, shares cost a lot more money than you receive in dividends. But you needn't worry! The purpose of investing is for the thing you invest in to be worth more in the future. That's why people often say 'invest in your future' – it means put a small amount towards your future now, so it can grow and be worth more later down the track.

Picture this: an airline is selling shares for $5 each. Each share is worth 1% of the business. You buy five shares for $25, and you now own 5% of the airline. At the end of the year, the airline has made a profit of $50. They pay you a dividend of $2.50 (5% of $50 = $2.50). (Not all companies will pay dividends. Dividends are paid when companies are not using the profits to re-invest in the business to support growth. If dividends are to be paid, a company will declare the amount of the dividend and all relevant dates.)

In ten years' time, the airline's shares are worth $15 each. You decide to sell your shares to someone else, and you make $50 on your investment ($15 × 5 = $75; you paid $25 for your shares, so $75 – $25 = $50), plus whatever dividends you received in the ten years you owned part of the airline.

An airline sells you 5% for $25

When the airline makes a profit, you get a dividend

If they keep making a profit, their shares are worth more

Which means you could sell them for a profit

An important caveat: there is always an element of risk when it comes to investing in shares. There is no guarantee that in ten years your shares will be worth more than you paid for them. Some shares are riskier than others. Often the bigger and more established a business is, the lower the risk. With lower-risk investments, however, the shares usually cost more because of the extra certainty, meaning you often don't make as much.

A smaller or newer business is often higher risk for the buyer because the business does not have as much history operating as a successful enterprise. However, in general, the higher the risk, the lower the cost. This means that if your shares are successful, you will get a larger return on your investment – your investment will be worth more.

A good rule to follow is to only invest what you can afford to lose.

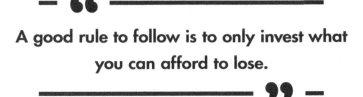

A good rule to follow is to only invest what you can afford to lose.

If you are counting on your shares as an investment to provide cash for a house in ten years' time – don't. Things can happen that no one sees coming (like Covid-19, for example), which may mean the business you have shares in is suddenly worth a lot less, and you end up losing money.

Of course, the opposite can happen too, and the worth of your shares may increase. But the point remains the same: don't put more into it than you can afford to lose. As you learn more about investing, you can take a few more calculated risks.

I choose to have higher-risk investments because I am young. I have longer in my life to make money, so I can afford to lose some if I make a bad call. When I first started to invest in shares a few years ago, I found it all a bit confusing. There are so many to choose from! And there are so many different places to buy shares. I found that the best place to start is a platform like Sharesies or Hatch. These platforms are great for beginners as they make investing very visual and simple to do.

There are two main types of shares you can buy: funds and businesses. Essentially, funds are a group of businesses. If you buy $10 worth of shares, your $10 investment is spread equally across the businesses in that fund group. When you buy shares in a business, your investment is only in that one business.

I invested in a mix of funds and businesses. Overall, I did okay. My total share portfolio is currently worth more than it was when I bought them all. But I went really wrong putting a large proportion of my investment into a business in the marijuana industry. It was right before the referendum on legalising marijuana here in New Zealand, and as we now know, that vote did not go the way I was hoping. The public said no. And my share value plummeted. Today, those shares are worth a lot less than when I bought them.

So what did I learn from this? That I'm not as smart as I think I am! I now try to stick to things that are lower risk, like funds.

The best thing, I think, is generally to buy shares and keep them for as long as possible. The short-term value of shares rises and falls within hours. Some people spend their lives buying and selling in short amounts of time to make money. But it takes years of experience to play the share market, and even then there will be losses. You may have heard that sometimes the share market 'crashes'. In short, this means that the value of shares plummets off the face of the earth. That said, after every crash in history, the share market has always eventually come back to exceed its previous value. So if you hold on to your shares long enough, they will most likely be worth more in the end. (Google it if you want – it's true!) Don't be scared off if your shares lose value or continually fluctuate – it's natural, and the last thing you want to do is lock in your losses by selling at a low point. Remember that you are in it for the long haul and stay away from trying to make a quick buck.

Compound interest

As you know by now, money sitting in a bank account earns interest, and you should aim to have your money in an account with no fees and the highest interest rate possible. Something you may not have heard about before is the magic of compound interest. Compound interest is the miraculous thing that happens when money in a high-interest bank account starts making money on the money it has already made. When you put your first deposit in a bank account, you have put in the 'principal' – the starting amount. This principal will start to earn interest. At the end of the month, your bank will pay interest into your account. You will now have the principal plus the interest. The next month, the interest will be calculated on this new amount, meaning that the interest you earned last month, the money that grew by itself, is now making even more money for you. And that's how you earn compound interest. (Paying it, on the other hand, sucks. You pay compound interest on things like mortgages, and it's basically the same idea, but you pay interest *to* the bank rather than them paying you.)

Compound interest is the miraculous thing that happens when money in a high-interest bank account starts making money on the money it has already made.

When you start out, chances are the compound interest you earn will be a very small amount. It might be so small that you question what the point is, so let's break it down so you can see how incredible compound interest really is.

Imagine you have a principal of $200. You add regular deposits to this account, say $200 every month. It won't look like much at the beginning, but at an interest rate of 1% p.a. you will have $84,195 in 30 years, and the interest you have earned will make up around 15% of that total ($11,995.58).

And that's just based on 30 years. If you are 20 and you start doing this now, at 60 you will have $118,276, with interest making up around 19% of that total ($22,076.61).

On the following page is a chart to show you the difference between how much you contribute versus how much interest you make on top of your deposits.

Did you notice how compound interest really started making its mark around year 15? From then on, the interest made up more and more of the total amount of money. Therefore:

- it's best to get started with compound interest as soon as you can
- it's a great way to have a nest egg ready when you retire.

To get your motor pumping, let's do another example: if you started off with a $5,000 principal and contributed

Compound interest

Years	Total contributions	Interest earnt (1%)	Future value
Year 0	$200.00	$0	$200.00
Year 1	$2,600.00	$13.04	$2,613.04
Year 2	$5,000.00	$50.32	$5,050.32
Year 3	$7,400.00	$112.09	$7,512.09
Year 4	$9,800.00	$198.58	$9,998.58
Year 5	$12,200.00	$310.06	$12,510.06
Year 6	$14,600.00	$446.77	$15,046.77
Year 7	$17,000.00	$608.96	$17,608.96
Year 8	$19,400.00	$796.89	$20,196.89
Year 9	$21,800.00	$1,010.81	$22,810.81
Year 10	$24,200.00	$1,251.00	$25,451.00
Year 11	$26,600.00	$1,517.71	$28,117.71
Year 12	$29,000.00	$1,811.21	$30,811.21
Year 13	$31,400.00	$2,131.77	$33,531.77
Year 14	$33,800.00	$2,479.66	$36,279.66
Year 15	$36,200.00	$2,855.15	$39,055.15
Year 16	$38,600.00	$3,258.53	$41,858.53
Year 17	$41,000.00	$3,690.07	$44,690.07
Year 18	$43,400.00	$4,150.06	$47,550.06
Year 19	$45,800.00	$4,638.77	$50,438.77
Year 20	$48,200.00	$5,156.51	$53,356.51
Year 21	$50,600.00	$5,703.56	$56,303.56
Year 22	$53,000.00	$6,280.21	$59,280.21
Year 23	$55,400.00	$6,886,77	$62,286.77
Year 24	$57,800.00	$7,523.53	$65,323.53
Year 25	$60,200.00	$8,190.80	$68,390.80
Year 26	$62,600.00	$8,888.88	$71,488.88
Year 27	$65,000.00	$9,618.08	$74,618.08
Year 28	$67,400.00	$10,378.73	$77,778.73
Year 29	$69,800.00	$11,171.12	$80,971.12
Year 30	$72,200.00	$11,995.58	$84,195.58

$1,000 a month with a 1% p.a. interest rate, in 30 years you would have a total of $426,376, and in 40 years you'd have $597,349.

Let's try something less conservative. Say you use term deposits to really get things moving. At the time of writing, these have a rate of around 6% p.a. Using roughly the same numbers, you will have $2,046,278 after 40 years (if the same interest rate continued – while this is likely to go up and down, it's good to get an idea using today's rates), and you will be earning around $118,496 per year on interest alone.

Google a compound interest calculator and run your own numbers to see what it can do! Put in realistic numbers and, remember, in the future you may be able to put in more than you can right now. But the trick is to get started. Start and don't stop till you hit your goal.

Term deposits

I briefly mentioned term deposits just now, so what the heck are those? Simply put, term deposits are accounts where you put your savings, just like in high-interest accounts, but you can't access the money because it is locked in. The bank will agree to give you a certain interest rate for your money over a set amount of time (normally from six months to five years), and during that time you cannot make any withdrawals. Because of this restriction, you are rewarded a much higher interest rate.

If you are now thinking about building up a large amount of savings using compound interest, term deposits are not a bad way to go, although you can't add money to a term deposit until the time period is up. This means you won't be able to get the full benefits of your added deposits until the term deposit ends and you are able to start a new one.

Weigh up the benefits and the timeframe. Use a compound interest and term deposit calculator to figure out what will work best for you. Remember, too, that you're usually required to deposit a minimum amount (typically around $5,000) into a term deposit.

KiwiSaver

KiwiSaver is a long-term investment scheme that most New Zealanders are part of. KiwiSaver supports you to save money for your retirement (and you can also withdraw from your KiwiSaver to help buy your first home).

When you start out in paid employment, you will fill in a form about KiwiSaver so that a portion of your wages is automatically deducted and paid into your KiwiSaver on payday. You won't see the money in your account, which removes any temptation to spend it. In most cases, your employer is also legally bound to add a minimum of 3% of your income to your KiwiSaver. This is on top of your current pay and is not deducted from what you are earning (although make sure you check the salary figure you are offered excludes KiwiSaver – if it doesn't, you may be on a lower base salary than you realise). Essentially if you opt in to KiwiSaver, you are giving yourself an instant 3% pay rise. Pretty smart work there, dudes!

You get to set the rate that you would like to contribute – at the time of writing, this can be 3%, 4%, 6%, 8% or 10%. As an added bonus, the government will give you an additional $521 each year as long as you have contributed at least $1,042. So if you only put in $1,042 (any way you like – it doesn't have to be through work), you will get a 50% return on your money. This is one of the easiest and most sure-fire investments you will ever make.

KiwiSaver is an investment because you are essentially investing in shares. KiwiSaver scheme providers look after your investment for you, and try to make you as much money as they can by making wise investments on your behalf. Not all scheme providers are equal – it's important to find the one that works best for you. Often people sign up to KiwiSaver through their bank. All KiwiSaver providers charge fees, and all will aim to give you a return on your investment.

As always, you want to get the highest return and pay the lowest fees possible. So do your research, my friends. There are a lot of providers out there, and some of the main ones with many customers (banks, for example) can easily charge high fees without working as hard to get you a good return on your investment. The banks and bigger providers will say they offer greater stability – but things change. There is competition out there, and that is GOOD for us! It means better deals.

When you choose a KiwiSaver fund, you will most likely have three options:

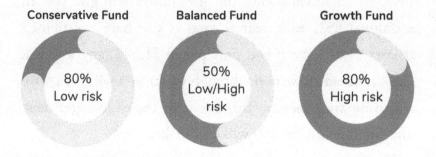

Conservative Fund	Balanced Fund	Growth Fund
80% Low risk	50% Low/High risk	80% High risk

1. A **conservative fund** has low-risk shares and will keep your investment as stable and protected as possible. Low risk also usually means low return.

2. A **balanced fund** is your 50/50 fund. Balanced funds are split between higher-risk and lower-risk investments.

3. A **growth fund** is mostly higher risk, but it also has the potential for higher returns.

It's a good idea to talk about your financial goals with a KiwiSaver advisor – often at the provider you are joining – to decide on a fund.

You can make a withdrawal from your KiwiSaver for only three reasons.

1. You are buying your first house.
2. You are retiring.
3. You are facing extreme financial hardship.

KiwiSaver can, in certain circumstances, help to buy a house. I will go into this further in Chapter 7, but in the meantime know that if you have been contributing to your KiwiSaver for a minimum of three years (36 months), you fall under the income-cap threshold and you're buying your first home, you might be eligible for a First Home Grant on top of being able to withdraw from your KiwiSaver. For an existing house, you could get $3,000–$5,000, depending on how many months you have been contributing, and you could get $7,000–$10,000 for a new build. If you're buying a house with someone else, and they are able to get a grant too, you could end up with $6,000–$20,000 added on. So it is worth starting to contribute soon – the sooner the better. Rack up those months, because if you've had KiwiSaver for three years but only contributed for one year, you will not qualify.

So plan what you are going to use your KiwiSaver for, pick the best fund and contribution rate for your circumstances, and start contributing. Simply go online, search 'KiwiSaver provider', find the right one for you, and sign up or transfer from your old one if you want to change. It's super easy. Most of the time you can just enter your details on the provider's website, and they will take care of the rest.

Offsetting your mortgage and lump sums

What do you do if you want to invest but you also want to pay off your mortgage? What's the best option? Good question, and not an easy answer.

Right now, Kaitlyn and I are focusing all our efforts and investing abilities towards paying off our mortgage. For us, it comes down to the numbers. It makes financial sense for us to put as much money towards our mortgage as possible because of current interest rates. Right now, if we were to put our money into something like a 12-month term deposit, we could get around 5.75% p.a. Not too bad, but we would need to pay tax on those earnings.

On the other hand, we are paying roughly 6.3% p.a. on our mortgage. The faster we pay this down, the less we will owe and the more we will be able to pay towards the principal rather than interest – and we won't be taxed on this.

To give you an example, if I pay off $10,000 of a $500,000 mortgage at 6.3% p.a. with a 30-year term, I will save $48,975 in interest and be one year and seven months closer to being mortgage-free. If I put $10,000 in a term deposit I will earn around $385 after tax in one year.

So that's $48,975 saved or $385 earnt – what would you choose?

> **Is it better to make a lump-sum mortgage repayment or put the money into a savings account or term deposit?**
>
> # 99% of the time
> ## a lump-sum mortgage repayment
>
> Interest rates on mortgages are almost always higher than the rates for savings accounts and term deposits. You'll not only avoid paying as much interest on your mortgage (which saves you $$$ in the long run), but you also won't pay tax on the interest saved (whereas you do pay tax on the interest you earn, if you had put the money in a long-term savings account).

You might then ask, well, where do I put the money while I'm saving this lump sum of $10,000? Not everyone has a sly 10k up their sleeves. And when do I pay the lump sum?

If you are saving a lump sum, you can put it in an offset account to save on interest as you pay down your mortgage in real time, all while still having your money available.

How does this work?

An offset account is an account that has a portion of your mortgage – normally fairly small – where you can also keep your everyday spending, savings or any other money. You still pay your mortgage repayments, but only towards the amount you *don't* have in the account. Say for example you have an offset account with $20,000 of your mortgage attached to it. If you have $5,000 in savings sitting in this account, you will only pay interest on $15,000 of your $20,000 mortgage. This is because the bank counts your savings as money you have paid back against your mortgage, even though it is still there and available to be used.

Exit strategy

Writing the term 'exit strategy' makes me think of the movie *Finding Nemo*. The cool turtle guy yelling at Marlin and Dory, 'DO YOU HAVE YOUR EXIT BUDDY?' Absolutely iconic.

If you are investing, you need to have an exit strategy. You can call it anything you like, but at the end of the day you need to have a plan in mind, an ultimate goal, so that you know what you are aiming for and when to act.

For example, if you are investing in KiwiSaver to build up a house deposit, your exit strategy is to use that investment when you have the right amount and you find the right house to buy. If you are contributing to your KiwiSaver for retirement, your exit strategy may be to draw it down when you retire so that you can fund your new-found love of golf.

An exit strategy is an acknowledgement of when you will stop investing and instead use the funds for your goal. It is important to have one to keep yourself on track, and when the market has ups and downs you will be less likely to have a knee-jerk reaction to it. The long game is nearly always the game you want to be playing, but it's not worth anything if you don't know when to pull out.

An exit strategy is an acknowledgement of when you will stop investing and instead use the funds for your goal. It is important to have one to keep yourself on track, and when the market has ups and downs you will be less likely to have a knee-jerk reaction to it.

Set a timeframe, a life-stage goal or something significant to mark when you will cash in your investments and use them for their purpose. It's good to remember that investments are meant to be used – they're not intended to be forever invested without any fun rewards. You might want to hold some investments for a rainy day or for your children, but make sure you set a point when you can reap some of the rewards too – you've earned it!

Chapter 5

The psychology of money

The pain of paying

Dun, dun, dun ... the psychology of money! Before you ask, no, I'm not a smarticle particle with a psychology degree who really understands how the mind works. I just like to learn about things and see how they relate to the real world. And I've found that a few nuggets about the psychology of money ring true.

First, let's talk about a guy named Ofer Zellermayer. Zellermayer has done some amazing research to help uncover why humans are so drawn to debt. He wrote his PhD on a concept he called 'the pain of paying', which refers to the negative emotions we experience when we pay for goods or services. The bigger the payment, the more painful it is. (It might not be just the fear of the dentist that makes you avoid getting your teeth checked!)

Humans are loss averse. We feel losses far more deeply than equivalent gains, and so we tend to go out of our way to avoid experiencing loss. Paying for something is a big loss and one we don't want to face, but at the same time buying stuff can give us a dopamine hit – aka pleasure! So our funky little brains are constantly trying to weigh up the pleasure of buying stuff versus the pain of paying for it.

And that's where debt comes in.

Parting with physical cash or our own funds on a card is psychologically far more 'painful' than using a method of delayed payment. Our brains see credit as the shining answer to the 'let's buy pretty things but yikes I have to pay for it' conundrum. Delaying payment by using a credit card, loan, or buy now, pay later scheme is far easier for our brains to handle. It just doesn't hurt as much. This could also be why buy now, pay later schemes are so popular with people who are perfectly able to pay the full cost upfront. Psychologically they feel like they are losing less, and so it hurts less. Basically they can just focus on the joy of their purchase in the moment.

In Chapter 3 I talked about how much I can't stand buy now, pay later schemes, and now we know why we like to use them. There is a similar scenario that is much better: pay now, buy later. By this I mean old-school layby – when you pay for something upfront in instalments until you own it, and then you can take it home.

Layby has a number of positives.

1. You are flexing your delayed-gratification muscle by not giving in to the need to have something straight away. You are likely being more intentional with your purchases – and it will feel a hundred times better.

2. You are not racking up debt. In a way you are being forced to save for an item, and you won't be able to spend the money while you save. The payments are broken down into affordable chunks that are pretty unnoticeable, and soon enough you own the item outright – no need for debt.

3. You won't be charged interest. If you set up a layby payment with a store, they will not charge you interest (most of the time). The store is not carrying any risk, therefore you don't need to pay for the risk. Yes, you will be missing out on any interest that you could be earning on your savings over this time, but if it is a smaller amount you may not have earnt much on it anyway, and this way there is no temptation to spend the money on something else.

I realise that layby will not work for everything. But when I bought wedding rings I had them on layby and paid them off over a year. I was so excited when I picked them up – I was proud that I had stuck to it and paid for them without incurring debt.

reminder:

buy now, pay later schemes thrive because of clever marketing tactics.

if you can afford the repayments, you can afford to pay upfront. it just takes a little planning ahead.

then you a) won't be in debt and b) will have so much more financial freedom in the following weeks.

While we associate parting with physical cash as *really* paying for something, swiping a card often doesn't quite have the same effect, does it? The numbers in our accounts don't feel as real as cold hard cash. I'd feel like a bloody baller if I had $1,000 in my hand (which never happens, btw), but when it's in my account it just doesn't feel like anywhere near as much. This is why I'm a fan of cash stuffing (see Chapter 1) – it helps every purchase feel *real*. And when it feels real, you are probably not going to want to touch it (or at least according to old mate Zellermayer).

Just a few months ago, I paid $35,000 cash for a car. On the one hand, I was super proud of myself for having the discipline to save that much money. On the other hand, handing that amount of cash over was brutal! It was the best, yet worst, feeling ever.

Man, look at me, making you feel like you should fear your money! I promise it's not all bad. In fact, there are so many ways to trick yourself into good money habits, and to feel good about intentional purchases and less good about debt. It all starts with being able to acknowledge your money. Really be honest with yourself about where you are at. And, yes, it's appropriate to say 'Yikes' right now.

That sly old dog, taboo

Sometimes I still question why I decided to be so open about money. I can feel a bit nervy talking about something as simple as writing a budget – it can create conflict, and has done before. Don't get me wrong: I love talking about debt and salaries and budgets and investments. I love talking with other people who are smashing through their money goals, and I'm so lucky that I hear these success stories all the time.

But when it comes to me personally, and the act of putting my finances out there, the whole thing can still give me the ick. And that's because of the sly old dog called taboo. A few years ago I read an article by Joe Pinsker in *The Atlantic* that put it down to the fear of judgement. Humans inherently want to belong, and judgement pushes us to the 'outside'. In cave-person days, the outside was not a safe place to be. Wealthy people might avoid talking about money because they feel guilty for being better off than those around them. If they don't talk about it, the guilt subsides and they don't have to face the realities of their place in an unequal society. Those with less money might also fear judgement because money is commonly linked (wrongly so) to someone's worth, their value as a person. Money taboos among people with less wealth are often considerably weaker, because people with less money typically aren't able to opt out of money conversations. Sharing information about money can be a powerful tool for survival for those on a low income.

Money taboos can be harmful in so many ways. Children who have grown up in families that sidestep money conversations might struggle to manage their expenses when they leave home. Elderly people might struggle to pay their bills in retirement and not know how to ask family members for help. An employee might think they're on a fair salary because they don't know how much their co-workers earn. If you weren't taught financial literacy as a child and money is taboo within your conversations as an adult, then this knowledge can be very hard to come by! Money taboos build walls between us, and can leave us feeling isolated and alone.

So how do we fix this? Should we immediately start announcing how much we earn at family dinners and firing questions at Aunt Pam about why she has four credit cards, then drown our awkwardness in boozy trifle? Perhaps not! But I do think that all of us here in our little 'budget-friendly' community are onto something. We're talking about money regularly, and this is surely a good thing. Telling someone about all your debt is no easy feat, but I get messages about this regularly. And once someone has taken a risk and broken the taboo, so many positive changes can come about. Honestly, hearing someone has paid off their debts because of a conversation we had is the absolute best feeling.

If someone in your life seems open to talking about money, go ahead and chat with them! It might feel a bit weird in the moment, but that's because we're not used to it. And if you don't know anyone irl who seems comfortable to talk, the wonders of the internet are available to help you out. Sometimes it's way easier to talk to a stranger about this stuff than someone you're close to. However you do it, go forth and have these hard conversations! Brick by brick, conversation by conversation, we can break down the taboo together.

The lifestyle creep

Writing out 'the lifestyle creep' makes me think of an old guy who stares at people in nice cars a bit too much. Fear not, this is not about him! The lifestyle creep is a silent phenomenon that happens as you earn more money: the more you earn, the more you spend. The 'lifestyle' creeps up on you.

I know quite a few people who should have it made but don't. They earn a lot of money and have done so for quite a while. You would think that they'd be paying off their mortgages, have no consumer debt and overall be just crushing it financially. Yet they are not. They have bigger debts and are living paycheque to paycheque, just the same as someone earning half what they do. Why?

When we earn less, we learn to make each dollar count because we have to. By the time we start to earn a bit more, it feels about time to loosen the purse strings a bit. So we start buying fancier bread, going on holiday each year and so on. Each time we start to earn more money, our lifestyle goes up with it, and we can stay in the same financial situation, relying on each paycheque albeit with some nicer things. But we will not really be getting ahead.

It is okay to spend more when you start to earn more, if it's intentional. But if you are starting to spend $100 more every week because you can, that's when it becomes a problem. I'll say it again: buy an income, not a lifestyle.

Make your money work for you. Buy investments that will result in another income stream or security for your future. Sure, spend $20 of that extra $100 a week on a few luxuries, but save the majority. You will thank me for it later if you do. After a while, when these investments start paying off, you will find that you are actually able to afford those holidays without relying on the paycheque cycle to keep you afloat.

Trick yourself into better habits

What can you do to help your funky little brain with money? Well, I'm not going to spout useless tips that tell you to 'be mindful' or 'be better' – if only our brains were programmed that way! Instead, here are a few sneaky tricks that might actually work when Uber Eats is calling even though the fridge is full.

1. The **24-hour rule** is a goodie to curb impulse spending. When you want to make a purchase, try waiting 24 hours instead of immediately throwing your credit card details at the checkout. After 24 hours, if you still want to buy the item and feel it's a good purchase to make, you can! This gives your brain a chance to find the dopamine hit you're craving elsewhere, and prevents you from impulse buying things that you don't really need.

2. Make a **'one in, one out' rule**: for every new purchase, commit to getting rid of, donating or selling a similar item you already own. This forces you to be more intentional when making purchases. We aren't above brute force here, pals.

3. Make it **hard to spend** your cash – get it out of reach of your toasty little mitts. Set up automatic transfers scheduled for payday to divert your money to accounts for bills and savings. If you know that you are someone who will just transfer the money straight back so you can buy another coffee, pop the money in an account with a lock on the gate, for example a 90-day notice saver, where you must give 90 days' notice to withdraw money. I have a slight suspicion that after 90 days, the impulse for that $5 coffee might have worn off!

4. **Reinforce positive habits** by surrounding yourself with positive influences. Reading this book is a great start. Now set up an environment that cheers you on. Follow encouraging and educational accounts on social media, read more books, talk to like-minded friends and family (internet friends count!), do a no-spend week (see page 148–150) – it all helps keep up your momentum.

5. Write an **okay sale list**. This little method allows some impulse spending but with limits in place.

Kind of like how clever people use rails at the bowling alley. Write down a list of things that have been on your mind for a while and are within your means. Then give yourself permission to buy these items if you see them on sale. When you see things on sale that are not on your list, remind yourself that they wouldn't be intentional purchases. This way, you can still feel like you're among the fun of buying things on sale, but you don't have to worry about going overboard or making impulsive decisions.

instead of:
impulse buying something the minute you see it.

try this:
write it down or take a photo of it. mull it over for a week. if it still 'sparks joy', then maybe it really will add value to your life.

I do a bit of a mix of all the above. Let's be honest, I am not perfect and neither are you! There will be plenty of times that we mess up and buy things we really don't need, and that's okay. We are humans, not robots – we are genetically bound to give in to impulses and cravings. I liken it to eating healthily. Everyone still wants chocolate once in a while, right? But if you keep yourself accountable and forgive the little mistakes, you will see progress. Consistency is the key, so don't be too hard on yourself.

reminder:

constantly buying stuff can be an emotional coping mechanism.

we don't actually need to buy stuff every day.

check in with yourself when you want to make a purchase.

do you feel bored? sad? lonely? stressed?

Money personalities

This is one of those times when we are going to talk about what box you fit in, like a BuzzFeed article that tells you what kind of drink you are (I'm a piña colada, fyi). And, I know, some of us just WON'T be put in a box, but thinking about your money personality is a great starting point to understanding who you are and where you want to go financially.

Even if your personality type isn't quite helping you thrive with money, there is hope. I used to be a real financial hot mess, and now ... okay, I'm still in the spender category. But my spending is a lot more considered and less frivolous!

One thing that can change your relationship with money more than anything is how much of it you earn. I know plenty of people who earn high six-figure salaries who are no better off than someone with a mid-five-figure income who has worked hard to save and achieve their goals. The more money you earn, the easier it is to live frivolously and not worry about money, but this does not lead to financial security. In fact, it can often lead to serious issues down the road. Imagine you have been spending thousands a week for years on end without saving as much as you should, unbothered about money in general because you have lots in the here and now. Then you lose your job. Or get sick. Or have children. How will you adjust? What's your backup plan? Most people who have survived on less will cope just fine – because they have always had to. Someone who hasn't will struggle a lot more and the reality checks will be harsher.

So what are the main money personalities? And which one are you?

1. Spenders: the ballers

Spenders love flash cars, having the latest tech and wearing Gucci clothing. They aren't exactly looking to find the clearance items. They want the best of the best and they're prepared to pay for it – even if it's not really within their means. They will always be on trend and like to have fun with their money. In terms of keeping up with the Joneses … they are the damn Joneses! They are not afraid of debt, credit cards or paying for items in ways that might make others shudder (can I hear a 'buy now, pay later'!).

Some people then get trapped in a cycle of spending money to feel better and then feeling guilty or remorseful afterward. They then spend more again to make themselves feel better.

2. Savers: the tightasses

Financial commitments, you say? Savers are all over that – to the extreme. They are the total opposite of spenders. They will yell at you to turn the lights off when leaving the room, close the fridge door as quickly as possible to keep in the cold, and shop only when needed and then on a strict budget. People who are savers can sometimes be seen as tightasses, as they're not always the first to offer to pay for something. They're not too concerned about following the latest trends; they get more satisfaction from seeing their KiwiSaver grow than buying a new phone. Savers are more conservative and don't take big risks with any investments.

3. Shoppers: the cash guns

Shoppers rely on spending money to get that big dopamine hit. They can't help but spend, even on things they don't need. They probably know they have a bit of a *problem* and worry about the choices they are making, but they'll easily get swept away when they next see a good bargain.

Shoppers may invest quite often, but their investments might not be too targeted. Often, for a shopper investing can give them a bit of a happy wave while making them feel less guilty about their other purchases. Other personality types might see investing as something for later, but for shoppers it's part of the spending deal.

Shoppers are similar to spenders, but they will spend more on bargains to avoid thinking about money, whereas spenders try to get as much cash as possible to buy big-ticket flashy items.

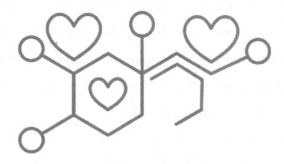

Shopping triggers the pleasure region of your brain and causes it to release dopamine.

4. Debtors: the plastic card surfers

Debtors aren't really trying to make big statements with purchases, or shopping to make themselves happy. They simply don't think about their money and don't know where it goes at the end of the day. Debtors live their lives paycheque to paycheque, just spending money without much thought. They tend to spend more than they earn and rack up high credit card bills and other debts. If all the credit and money runs out, and shit hits the fan, that's when debtors can find themselves in hot water.

5. Investors: the block builders

Investors are aware of their money. They know exactly how much comes in and when it goes out. They have a total handle on their financial situation. They are planning for their future and set goals to ensure that their money works for them. They will seek passive income streams and investments that will pay off in the long term. Investors are careful with their decisions and understand the need for some risk in their investments. They will ensure all their bills are paid on time and that any other income goes towards their goals.

In my view none of these money personalities is ideal. I think your best chance of financial health comes with balance. You need a bit of the spender and shopper in your life, and a bit of the tightass and investor. Maybe not so much the debtor though, eh?

Why do I say that? Well, let's look at the likely future of each personality type.

The spender buys big-ticket items that lose value fast and leave them without a secure future. They might not have the same level of income forever – what happens if it goes down?

Saver: okay, great. They've spent as little as possible and put everything away for a future that comes … when? At what point will they be happy? When will they have saved enough? And when will they be able to spend it? Where does the joy come in?

Shoppers will have to face the music one day. Yes, they have invested, which is great, but in what? Did they think it through? Even if they've made good investments, will it be enough to save them from their shopping habits? Probably not.

Debtor: this one is obvious. Does bankruptcy sound fun?

The investor has done everything right. All by the book. They've calculated the heck out of life and taken good risks. Some have paid off, and they are probably going to be very secure. But again where is the joy? Are you not human?

My point is – it's all about making sure there is balance.

This is why I talk about having a realistic budget: one that works on having lower bills, higher income, less spending and more saving money. You need to have joy in your life. You need to be allowed to be human, or else what's the point? I know you may have another view on this. You might also have no choice when it comes to the odd splurge – your situation may just not allow for it, and that's okay. The thing I want you to take from this is that there is no one set way that's best. It's a combination – aim for that. Not perfection.

Chats

It's time for chats with you guys! At the start of this chapter, I mentioned that talking about money helps to break down taboos and shed light on what is possible. I have had the privilege of conducting interviews with some awesome humans and we have chatted about money, where they're at and how they feel about it. The first chat I want to share is with

Le Anna, whom I spoke with in January 2023. She is a total OG to the mahi I have been doing and was wonderful to talk to.

LE ANNA

Le Anna, her partner and their three young children live in their own home in Ōtorohanga, around 50 kilometres south of Hamilton. They live pretty comfortably, budgeting carefully and being very intentional with their money. They're happy with where they are financially, but it was a big journey for them to reach this place. Le Anna's partner was made redundant during the Covid-19 pandemic, just before their second baby was due to arrive.

Income

I'm not currently in paid work due to having three young children. My partner earns $1,300 each week after tax. He's a project manager for a construction company in Hamilton. We also get $468 in Working for Families Tax Credits each fortnight.

Expenses

Our mortgage is split into two different parts on two different interest rates. Combined they work out to around $750 a fortnight.

We budget around $200 for groceries a week and often come in under. This is because we bulk up and stretch out our meals as much as we can. We have a quarter of a beast in the freezer, so we really only buy chicken from the supermarket.

Childcare is $80 per week. Our daughter is four, so she gets 20 free hours. When our two-year-old turns three, she'll get 20 free hours too, which will help bring the cost down.

Transport-wise, my partner's vehicle is completely covered by his job. They pay for fuel and servicing. We just pay for any big personal trips, like when we visit family in Whanganui. With my car, the cost varies, especially if we're driving into Hamilton a lot. Typically I spend about $70 per week on fuel.

My partner's phone is also covered by his work. For my phone, I chose the cheapest prepaid plan at $10 per month. This gives me unlimited texts, some minutes and not much data. But I've found that plenty of places have free public Wi-Fi if I need it while I'm out. Otherwise I don't really need much data anyway because I'm busy with the kids.

I also spend $7 per week on health insurance. This is hands-down the best investment I've ever made. I wasn't taking care of my health as much as I should have been, but since getting health insurance I've felt like I can justify it. They cover 75% of GP appointments, dental visits, contact lenses, etc. It's great!

I also budget $9 per month for a Patreon subscription. I have a second subscription too, but this one is covered by what I get from running my own Patreon.

Including our mortgage, all our bills come to around $1,450 per fortnight. This includes all of the above (except groceries), plus life insurance, rates, water and our $19 Spotify subscription.

Debt

We don't have any specific debt aside from our mortgage. We bought both of our cars outright, the second one using money from the sale of our previous home.

Occasionally I'll use Afterpay if I want to stagger big purchases. This saves me from messing up my budget too much and having to do multiple transfers. I've never gotten in trouble with it, however, and am very responsible about using it. For example, for Christmas last year we spent around $300 on gifts and paid this off over the next four to five weeks. We tend to pay the first automatic payment and then manually pay off the rest sooner than the automatic deductions.

Savings

We have shared household savings of $2,900, which cover family stuff like takeaways. Basically anything that's not a bill. Our groceries come out of this account too. This kinda helps as motivation, because the less we spend on groceries, the more we can do as a family.

For personal savings, I have $1,500 and my partner has $1,600. We both put $100 into our personal savings accounts each pay cycle. My partner mostly spends his on food for his lunches, and mine tends to be spent either on fuel or food too.

Investments

My partner's KiwiSaver is currently sitting at $20,000, and mine is at $1,000. This is because we put it towards buying our home and I haven't been in paid work since.

What would you do if you needed money in an emergency?

This would come from our other savings; we like to have a buffer in our accounts. My partner also has life and income-protection insurance, so that could help depending on the emergency.

How would you describe your financial situation?

It's comfortable to a point. We don't stress about money but only because we are very intentional with our finances. We make ongoing, specific choices to keep us in this position. For example, with the cost of living going up hugely, we cancelled subscriptions, and we are always looking for new ways to stretch meals. We also borrowed far less than the maximum we could get for our mortgage, because we knew that interest rates would probably rise and we wanted to maintain our lifestyle. We feel relatively comfortable money-wise because of our efforts to be conscious and intentional, alongside our privileges in life. In saying that, however, we don't feel comfortable enough to not be looking at costs or finding ways to cut them.

Needing to have a good grasp on money stems from my CPTSD (complex post-traumatic stress disorder). This would make me anxious, panicked and stressed about everything. My trauma, interestingly enough, actually taught me good money habits. I needed them to get through it.

Do you feel in control of your finances?

Yeah, definitely. I tend to know what's going out on what days, and have rough account balances in my head.

Do you worry about money?

Not much anymore. I worry a little about day-care costs, because we have a minor disagreement with WINZ (Work and Income New Zealand) going on. Our most recent water bill was also $50 higher than we anticipated, so that took us by surprise. Overall, we don't worry much though because we have buffers in place and try to make the most of what we already have.

Any money regrets?

Yes! My first car. I set a budget, took out a loan from the bank, and maxed it out without doing research first. I got a VW Polo, which of course ended up costing more to fix than it was worth. I paid $5,200 for it, plus interest, plus $3,000 in repairs. Eventually I traded it in for parts and got $200 out of it.

I also regret not setting clear financial boundaries in previous relationships. It meant that I've lost out on a lot of time that could've been spent saving for my future and learning to manage my own money better.

What was money like growing up?

We didn't talk about it much. My family moved overseas because they could earn more on just one wage than here in New Zealand. They earnt a decent amount but would spend a lot, and not really keep money aside as a backup.

Toughest financial situation

This would have to be when I was 18. I'd just moved back to New Zealand after living overseas with my family. It was the first time I'd lived outside my family home, and I decided to go flatting. I hadn't found a job yet and only had $2,500 sitting in my account. There were a few weeks of 'Shit! I'm going to run out of money!' until I got a job. It was pretty stressful.

Proudest financial moment

Right now I'm feeling pretty proud. We're on top of our money right now. A year ago our savings were zero. But we built them up slowly, adding $50 a week. It was pretty cool when they hit four figures. Being able to purchase our car outright was cool too. It's a good feeling.

Best financial advice

When you're sorting out your budget, take it one step at a time. Don't try to cut everything out all at once. It's kind of like when you're trying to eat healthy or start exercising. Just pick one thing to focus on, and get that sussed first. Like, if you're overwhelmed with your money, pick a debt to pay off first. Then the next. Then focus on saving. Your chapter one might be somebody else's chapter five, so don't compare. Just start small and focus on what you're doing.

> **— 66 ——**
>
> **Just pick one thing to focus on, and get that sussed first. Like, if you're overwhelmed with your money, pick a debt to pay off first. Then the next. Then focus on saving. Your chapter one might be somebody else's chapter five, so don't compare.**
>
> **—— 99 —**

How do you think most other Kiwis are doing financially?

I reckon most are struggling hard. Probably more than we realise – some people are definitely too proud to say they are struggling. I also reckon that some people don't realise that they can change their money habits. If you're complaining that you have no money, but then you're going to concerts all the time and stuff, well, that's on you.

Where do you want to be financially?

Our biggest goal is to buy some land and live as sustainably as we can. This is coming from a big place of privilege. We'd love to be in the position where we have excess produce to share. I'd also love to be in a place where we can buy the things that matter to us. Like ethical peanut butter instead of whatever is cheapest! I'd like to buy locally without destroying the bank. Basically, just being able to live in a way that aligns with our values.

ABBY

Abby (not her real name) is 19 years old and lives in the city in a rented cabin on her brother's property. She recently moved there to lower her living costs and be closer to work. She has a cat and likes to live a fairly social lifestyle.

Income

I make around $1,600 a fortnight after tax working 39 hours a week as a pharmacy/retail assistant and make-up counter manager.

Expenses

Every fortnight I spend $260 in rent, $150 to $200 in petrol and about $100 to $150 on groceries. My car insurance is $40.

My spending really depends on my mood and can fluctuate a lot. I can end up spending anywhere from

$100 to $800 on shopping, eating out and just life in general.

Debt

I owe my mum $250 and have a couple of parking tickets that are $85 each. These are about to become overdue and have extra fines added to them. I don't have any other debt or credit cards or anything.

Savings

I don't have any savings because things seem to keep popping up. My car breaks a lot! I would like to save $10,000 for a new car by the end of winter 2024. I want to try saving $750 a fortnight after Christmas onwards.

Investments

I don't have any investments. It would be nice to have them in the future, but I don't really feel like I know enough about investing to get into it.

What would you do if you needed money in an emergency?

I would go to family and ask them to help me. That's what I have done in the past, and then I try to pay them back as soon as I can.

How would you describe your financial situation?

I'm definitely more than comfortable with the amount of expenses I have compared to how much I make. I can very easily live off it and save. But I do end up spending my money in the wrong places, which makes me feel like shit because at the end of the day I have nothing to show for my money.

Do you feel in control of your finances?

I could definitely be more in control! I feel like I can pay for things, so I don't stress about it, but I want to be better and stick to a budget.

Do you worry about money?

Sometimes – when I think about everything that I have to pay for, and the money I have at the time, it overwhelms me. For example, the number of things that need to be fixed on my car – it's a lot and I just put it off.

Any money regrets?

Not saving at least a small portion of my money consistently. If I did, things would be a lot better now. I also always regret spending money on unnecessary things.

What was money like growing up?

I never really knew a lot about money. My parents split when I was very young. Mum and I wouldn't really talk about money and when she was struggling, at the time, I didn't know. With my dad, I always thought he had a lot of money. The older I got, the more I learnt the value of money, because the more obvious it was seeing Mum struggle and seeing how other families lived compared to us. But at the end of the day, I also knew that I never actually had to worry about it, which was comforting – I knew that they would keep me safe.

Toughest financial situation

For me it would just be when I need to get my car fixed and I don't have the money for it. I'm not really too stressed about it as I know it could be a lot worse, but it's not fun having that hang over me.

Proudest financial moment

I was saving for a car (ironically the one I have now), and nearly had enough when I found the one I liked. When I bought it, I borrowed the remainder of the money I needed from my brother but was then able to pay back the amount I owed him within two weeks.

Best financial advice

The best advice that I would give would be to save at least 10% of your paycheck and actually think about things before you buy them. And yes, I know how hypocritical that is.

The best advice that I would give would be to save at least 10% of your paycheck and actually think about things before you buy them. And yes, I know how hypocritical that is.

How do you think most other Kiwis are doing financially?

I know that a big portion of Kiwis are struggling with money, but I also know there is a big percentage that are comfortable or well off. For the majority – I think they are struggling and likely underpaid.

Where do you want to be financially?

For right now, I want to be able to pay for the things I need to, like my car, and save a decent amount before I move out of where I am now. I would also like to get a well-paid job after this job to start my career and give my finances a boost.

JESSICA

Jessica (not her real name), her partner and their daughter live rurally on the North Island with several large dogs and many cats. They moved there from the city in search of a better quality of life. Jessica uses aids to walk and she's in and out of a wheelchair.

Income

I am a supported-living beneficiary. My partner is too because he is my carer. We both work part-time – me with my business and my partner gardening – with varying incomes from this. I started my business due to my illness, so that I could work from home on my phone. We only 'rely' on our set weekly supported-living payments due to how our part-time work fluctuates.

Expenses

Our mortgage is $248 per fortnight. We have standard bills like power, internet and our mobile phones. These are all on the cheapest rates. We also have some old debts that we're paying off weekly. We pay less for power in winter than other families, as we have a wetback water heater, and we don't pay for water because we're on a tank. We set money aside into sinking fund categories like birthdays, Christmas, daughter, car, medical, pets and savings. I'm sure there are more!

There's a quote that really resonates with me that describes our relationship with our expenses at this stage. It goes something along the lines of: if you don't have enough to cover all the loose ends, then work on having fewer loose ends instead.

There's a quote that really resonates with me that describes our relationship with our expenses at this stage. It goes something along the lines of: if you don't have enough to cover all the loose ends, then work on having fewer loose ends instead.

Debt

We have $16,000 in debt. Some of this is old, defaulted debts that my partner racked up when he was younger. He also has student loans. We've just finished paying off our car, and our mortgage is currently at $67,000.

Savings

We have approximately $5,000 in savings. About $3,000 of this is set aside for house maintenance, $1,000 in general savings and the rest is spread across our sinking funds.

Investments

I withdrew all of my KiwiSaver to purchase our property – there's nothing left in there. My partner has around $2,000 in his. We would both like to contribute to our KiwiSavers more, but neither of us has had stable work since we purchased our property.

What would you do if you needed money in an emergency?

We'd use our savings. But to be honest, depending on the emergency, we'd often try to solve it ourselves first. If we can cover it by cutting back for a few weeks, fixing it ourselves or living without, then we will. Although we're beneficiaries, we can't get advances from WINZ because our cash assets are too high, so we don't use this option.

How would you describe your financial situation?

Getting by … just. We have enough savings to stop us falling flat, but no ability to increase our income in any significant way.

Do you feel in control of your finances?

We control our finances to the cent. But I feel like the real control lies out of our power. We are at the mercy of life, messy and unplanned as it is.

Any money regrets?

Yeah, getting debts while we were younger. My partner defaulted on a lot of payments and I racked up consumer debt. We paid off my debt to purchase our property but are still working on his.

I also wish I'd bought my home sooner. We chose to move from the city to the country, and our quality of life has improved significantly, plus by owning our home we're working on an asset of our own. Our home cost $120,000, but if we'd done it sooner our property would have been cheaper.

What was money like growing up?

We both come from single-parent households with low incomes and large amounts of consumer debt. I personally took responsibility for the family finances at a young age as my mother died when I was in my teens. I was on my own with no backup. You learn quickly when there's no backup.

Toughest financial situation

Before we decided to move to the country, we were stuck in a one-bed flat under someone's home with a small baby. It got no sun at all and cost heaps. We were both miserable and felt like we were drowning.

Proudest financial moment

Holding the keys to our home for the first time!

Best financial advice

Just keep picking yourself up, even if you get it wrong. Even when you've 'failed' and when there's no light at the end of the tunnel. Budgeting isn't about money; it's about resilience.

How do you think most other Kiwis are doing financially?

I think a lot of people are struggling. I also think a lot of people are putting on a brave face.

Where do you want to be financially?

I want to pay off my home, sell it and move into a bus with land to park it on. We'd like to be as off-grid as possible.

SOPHIE

Sophie is a single mum living with her four-year-old daughter in Avondale, Auckland. She has just started a new full-time job as a customer service manager after being on a benefit during her daughter's early years. Sophie has recently experienced a huge change in how she manages her money. Her old 'bury my head in the sand' approach is now out the window and she's saving to buy a home for herself and her daughter.

Income

I feel like most people don't see the reality of what many solo parents survive on. Up until starting my new job, I received $730 in benefits from WINZ and $36 in Working for Families Tax Credits per week. My ex paid child support, but this would go straight to the government to go towards the sole-parent support that I received. It was an incredibly tight time for my daughter and me. Something as small as a flat tyre could sweep us under.

With my new job, I'm on $75,000 per year and I'm paid $1,075 per week after tax. This is a huge jump up from what we lived on while on the benefit, and it will change our lives. Although I'd like to be at home with my daughter while she's small, I have to go to work so that we can afford to live.

Expenses

I have a spreadsheet that tracks my income and expenses every single week. Right now, our expenses are approximately $924 per week. Rent is $450 per week for a two-bedroom unit, which includes water. We don't have a washing machine, so I spend $15 per week at the laundromat. My phone is $50 per month, internet is $65 per month, and petrol is about $60 per week. My daughter and I are both lactose-intolerant, and I'm also gluten-free, so our grocery budget each week is $120. Day care costs $120 per week too. I have a personal loan from my dad, which was to purchase my hybrid car, and I pay him back $50 per week. I have a Patreon membership, which costs $10 per month. This is really important to me because this community is my village.

I manage all these expenses by setting small amounts of money aside each week so that I'm not hit with big bills as the costs arise. For example, each week I put aside $15 for my phone and $30–$40 for power (which is cheaper as I pay in advance with Powershop). I also set aside $50 each week for insurance (contents, car and health, which means we can claim back GP visits, allergy tests, etc.).

Before I began my new job, our expenses were greater than my income. They were about $774 per week, which was just a smidge over the $766 that would be in my account each week. We were living paycheque to paycheque and had literally zero wiggle room. We couldn't afford for anything to go wrong.

Debt

My only debt is the personal loan that I got from my dad. He doesn't charge me interest – I'm very lucky! I paid off and cancelled my credit card about four months ago. This was when I had a big reality check with my finances and started using a spreadsheet to budget. My credit card kept me stuck in a cycle. Now I'm able to put any extra money towards our savings rather than credit card repayments.

Savings

I have $1,100 in a savings account.

Investments

My KiwiSaver is currently sitting at $30,700. Before my daughter was born, I was contributing to it at 8% because my expenses were minimal. This will now continue to grow because of my new job.

What would you do if you needed money in an emergency?

Honestly, I'd ask my parents or my sister. My parents weren't in a position where they could help for a long time, as they had six kids at home when I was growing up. It was very hard for them to make ends meet. My dad worked two jobs and my mum was sick for a long time, before eventually being able to work on the weekends. Now they don't have any kids at home and are in a far more stable financial position.

How would you describe your financial situation?

It has been so stressful. I think about money every single day. I'm so aware of the impact it has on me and my daughter.

Do you feel in control of your finances?

Yes! Ever since I started using spreadsheets to track my money and budget, I've felt in control. Before all of that, back when I had a credit card, I just wouldn't look. I've since realised that I need to get it all sorted out, as I want to buy a house in the next 12 to 24 months. This is the goal that I'm working towards, so having control over my money is crucial.

Any money regrets?

The biggest one would be my wedding. I have endometriosis and felt a lot of pressure to rush into marriage and have kids because I wasn't sure what would be on the cards in the future. So I ended up getting married at 23 and we spent $20,000 on the big day. In hindsight that was an awful lot of money, especially considering our relationship didn't work out. I don't regret our honeymoon, though.

I'd like to get married again one day, but would want a very low-key 'within-our-means' wedding. We'd have a quiet ceremony, and then everyone would bring a plate to share after, you know?

What was money like growing up?

It was pretty tough, but I didn't fully realise the extent of it at the time. My parents worked so hard to make life fun and to keep the family afloat. We'd make Christmas presents ourselves and stuff. My mum struggled to feed everyone until my older siblings left home. It's only since I've become a parent myself that I can appreciate how hard it was for them.

Toughest financial situation

During Covid-19 I got into both credit card and personal loan debt. I had to borrow money from my daughter's future account because the interest was too high, and I couldn't meet repayments otherwise. I never want to do that again. I've since repaid her account and I'm so glad that she'll have a safety net growing up.

Proudest financial moment

Getting my new job. I went into the interview with the absolute maximum confidence. I asked for $75k per year, and I got it! I don't have to rely on my daughter's dad at all, and we can save for a house. I'm so proud to be fully supporting myself and my daughter.

Best financial advice

Do a spreadsheet every single week. It changed my life. Do the spreadsheet even if it's uncomfortable and annoying. I started doing this about four months ago, after seeing a post in the Patreon group I'm part of, which totally revolutionised how I deal with money. I put all my income and expenses into a spreadsheet for the first time and saw that I wasn't making ends meet. I was burying my head in the sand, especially with my credit card. I also realised that I couldn't get anywhere being on a benefit.

Having a big goal can also help. On top of doing a spreadsheet, I've started making goals and planning how to reach them. I changed the name on my bank account to 'house deposit'. That means if I want to spend some money on dinner or something, I think twice because I'm literally taking it out of my house deposit.

How do you think most other Kiwis are doing financially?

I think we're all struggling. Food, clothes, petrol, rent, everything! It's so tough.

— 66 ——

I changed the name on my bank account to 'house deposit'. That means if I want to spend some money on dinner or something, I think twice because I'm literally taking it out of my house deposit.

—— 99 —

Where do you want to be financially?

I'd like my daughter and me to be in our own home. I'd also like to be able to fund myself creatively. I write poetry and have also started my own Patreon to tell my coming-out story. I'd love to be able to build this up to a full-time income.

Try it for yourself

I find listening to everyday New Zealanders tell their financial stories so interesting. And I think that's because we don't talk about this stuff. I bet you found their stories interesting too. I would guess that you didn't think negatively towards these people or their situations. If anything, they might have inspired you or made you feel less alone. And that's the true power of sharing.

I talked a lot earlier about breaking money taboos by talking about our finances. I hope that in reading these stories you can see that it's not as scary as it seems, and only good things will come from it. You might find that you learn a great trick someone else is doing that will help you too. You could gain a new perspective or outlook on your situation. It might also give you a reality check – let's be honest, we all need one sometimes.

Try it out. Chat to people about money! If the first person you go to isn't open to sharing, try someone else. Keep going and make the conscious decision to have these conversations. We'll all be better for it.

Chapter 6

Money challenges

By now, you know there are a lot of different things you can do with your income and expenses to have a positive effect on your day-to-day finances. But have you ever tried a money challenge? The aim of the game is to set some type of goal and achieve it within a small timeframe. I'm not talking about big, lofty goals like paying off the mortgage – you want small, achievable goals that will boost your motivation and send you on your journey towards a bigger goal. Money challenges can be good to do with family or friends – you could even make it into a competition.

The no-spend week

Okay, don't take the name of this one too literally. A no-spend week (or fortnight or month – however long you like) is a predetermined time period you set for yourself, or your family, when you won't spend any money aside from covering essential bills. This means no takeaways, no lunch dates, no movies, etc. You only spend money on the things in your budget – nothing more.

Kaitlyn and I like to do these to rein ourselves back in after a period of big spending, where we might have been splurging or there might have been a load of unexpected costs. Whatever the reason, a no-spend week is a great way to hit the reset button and see the bank account looking a bit healthier.

what our family does during a no-spend week

Try out new online recipes

Swim at the beach (ever day if we can!)

Visit local libraries

Have a games night

Movies and microwave popcorn

Neighbourhood scavenger hunts

Visit friends and have playdates

Playground afternoons

Declutter things we don't need

No-spend weeks are also a great way to bring mindfulness to your spending. As soon as you finish a no-spend week, you will likely find that spending money on nonessentials will be a lot more noticeable, and you will be a lot more mindful about it.

The declutter

Who doesn't love a good declutter? You might think of decluttering as going through old boxes and finally parting with the Barney the dinosaur soft toy that has been around since you were three. Budget-friendly declutters are a chance to pull things from around the house that can be exchanged for cold, hard cash, baby.

Search your house to find things you no longer need that are still in usable condition (no used underwear, please). Sort them into two piles: one for things you think you can sell, and one for unsellable items. With your first pile, have a garage sale, or chuck the items up on Facebook Marketplace to skip seeing awkward people look at your unwanted things in front of you. PSA: a bunch of scammers will contact you on Facebook Marketplace, so there is that. But, hey, it's free.

With your second pile, and anything else that doesn't sell from your first pile, donate the items to an op-shop or offer them for free on your local community page. Please don't take rubbish to op-shops – don't be that guy.

I try to have a declutter every six months or so. They're a great way to make sure you only have things in your house you use or want to hold on to, and they make that back corner of the garage feel less like a dumping ground.

The 30-day savings goal

Write down how much money you want to save in the next 30 days. Now break it up into 30 chunks of all different sizes. Then, every day for 30 days, 'spend' one of these amounts on your savings.

30 days, $200

$1	$5	$10	$15	$20
$8	$3	$15	$1	$5
$2	$5	$6	$2	$1
$5	$4	$9	$1	$12
$5	$1	$3	$18	$2
$4	$11	$5	$20	$1

For example, if you want to save $200 in 30 days, one chunk might be $35, another might be $5. All 30 chunks will add up to $200, and each day you can choose a chunk and contribute that amount to your savings. At the end of the 30 days, you will have saved $200! Go you.

Lots of people find this technique works for them because saving smaller chunks is more manageable and less noticeable than saving bigger chunks.

The hustle goal

This one's for the creative people who want to dive into something and just have fun with it.

See how much money you can make outside your usual income. First, set a target amount that you want to earn over 30 days. (For this challenge to work, you need to be realistic about how much time you can commit. If you only have a few free hours a week, make sure to set a lower target. If you can commit an hour or two a day, set something higher.) Next you need to hustle. Find any and every way to make money. You don't need big wins or a well-thought-out plan – there's no room for doubt in 30 days! Just jump straight in. Offer to mow lawns, weed gardens or wash cars. Jump on freelance websites to see what work you could pick up. Go to op-shops and find something to restore and on-sell. Do anything you can to make a bit of extra money.

I like to do this challenge with someone. The competition can be so much fun. When Kaitlyn and I did it, we decided to flip furniture. I made about $600 and she made about

$250. I was pretty pleased with myself and I *tried* not to be a sore winner, but it was hard.

The thrifty 30

For this challenge, it's all about spending as little as possible on everything for 30 days. And I mean EVERYTHING. See if you can get away with not using the car so you spend less on fuel. Take lunch to work or school rather than buying anything. Don't go out. Don't buy new clothes. If you have to buy something, go secondhand – find a bargain. Find free things to do on the weekend and make your own entertainment. Act like every single dollar is a dollar you won't spend. Be that guy. Have fun with it!

Keep yourself on track by inviting a friend to join you and seeing who can spend the least across the month (the loser has to shout the winner lunch at the end of the challenge).

Sustainable economic thinking

You might think that living in a sustainable way is an expensive luxury, but it doesn't have to be. I have had a lot of conversations with my mate Kate Hall, aka Ethically Kate, on the topic of budgets and sustainability, and there are so many ways that living sustainably can save you money.

sustainability and budgeting often go hand in hand

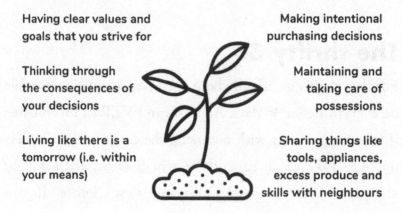

Having clear values and goals that you strive for

Making intentional purchasing decisions

Thinking through the consequences of your decisions

Maintaining and taking care of possessions

Living like there is a tomorrow (i.e. within your means)

Sharing things like tools, appliances, excess produce and skills with neighbours

Learning to fix and repair things rather than immediately replacing them

I am not going to tell you that you need to rush out and get a bento box (although they are great), buy stainless-steel pegs, and remove everything plastic from your life. This would actually not be very sustainable at all, although a lot of people on Instagram would have you think that's the only way to go.

A sustainable money challenge can be as simple as cutting down on waste and single-use items, or being more mindful about where you spend your money. If something's broken, try to repair it rather than replace it. Here are a few ideas of sustainable challenges to get you started.

Start composting

Composting is a great way to remove food scraps from your waste. Don't pay to throw them away – let them compost and have another life in your garden! When we started composting, I discovered that at least half our waste was coming from food scraps. (No, we don't force our kids to finish their plates and we don't say things like, 'Do yOu kNow hOw lUCky yOu aRE?!')

It's very easy to start composting. If you don't want to buy a brand-new compost bin, look for a secondhand one or just make your own! All you need is a corner in your garden (if you have the space) – just ensure the compost is covered and protected from pests. Read up on composting, and then when it's ready you will have beautiful, rich soil you can use to grow your own veggies!

Grow your own food

Composting leads perfectly to growing your own food – this, too, does not have to cost much. If you have space for a garden, mark it out and turn the soil. You could have pots or raised veggie beds, or even pick up an old, lead-free bathtub to grow your plants in! (You could use your new compost to fill it up.) Google will tell you when to plant what and how to look after it. You don't even need to buy seeds from the shop – many of the fruit and veggies you are already buying at the supermarket will have seeds you can use. (Some need to be dried out and stored for later use, and some are ready to go! Again, Google can tell you what to use when.)

Use eco-transport

I am a bit of a sucker for electric cars. They make sense financially but are also great for the environment. I don't own one yet, but I can see one very clearly in my future. For now, to save money and the planet, I:

- walk or bike as much as possible
- catch public transport
- plan out my trips so I use fuel efficiently
- keep the car in its 'eco' mode (hoping this actually does something)
- car pool.

There are fewer eco-transport options when we all go out as a family so we often use the car, and that's okay! We just do what we can, when we can. It all adds up.

When you shop, go secondhand

Okay, so if you are anything like I used to be, you'll have to politely hear me out for this bit. If you are like my wife, I'll be preaching to the choir. Shopping at op-shops is quite a new thing for me. In fact, only about a year ago I had a heated debate with a good friend about how I wouldn't shop at op-shops because I could never find anything I liked. I was convinced there was nothing worth having at an op-shop. People only donate old stuff no one wants, otherwise they would sell it, right?

Wrong. Obviously.

I grew up going to op-shops with my aunty. She'd pick up amazing bargains and use them for her business. (She runs an eco-clothing brand.) She would go for items she knew people would pay good money for and sell them on for a profit – it was incredible. All I saw were random clothes! She still sources a lot from op-shops, using materials to create new garments to sell in her shop. So how on earth did I end up thinking there was nothing in an op-shop worth keeping? Why did I have the frankly embarrassing opinion that only people who couldn't afford new stuff would go there? Why the stigma?

I think I can trace it back to my childhood (therapy session, here we come). When I was younger, my parents ran a very successful restaurant. My dad is an award-winning chef and my mum is one of those amazing people who can do anything she turns her hand to. She ran the customer service side of the restaurant and balanced all the books. I never knew at the time that we were well-off. If anything, I thought we were pretty poor – we never went on holidays and we were not spoiled kids. But we had everything we needed and were very comfortable. Now I know my parents paid off their mortgage and business loan in a few years, and saved up and paid for the whole house to be renovated using cash. They drove nice cars and could afford nice things for me and my four siblings.

Cut to when they separated. I was 11. Over the next few years I finally realised what money was worth. I saw the difference between having it and not. Because of a drawn-out divorce settlement, my mum started from scratch. My siblings and I would stay with each parent for a week at a time. Staying with Dad, we were in the family house with all the comforts we were used to. Staying with Mum, we started off in my aunty's lounge. We then moved to a rental with three bedrooms. Most of the furniture and essentials had been donated to us. It was cold and cramped. My mum took a lot of odd jobs – some that had her working all hours, some that paid her barely enough to cover the bills. She managed to move to a bigger house, but then work dried up and Mum was on the benefit. It was not enough to live on – not by a long shot. There was one Christmas when we were lucky enough to be selected for an 'angel' Christmas, where those in need receive Christmas presents and food. Mum was cleaning houses and doing whatever she could to bring in money. She applied for jobs constantly but with no luck for a long time. I watched Mum work her money to the last cent. She'd show me how $300 would get our large family enough groceries for a full fortnight.

Nothing was bought that wasn't intentional. No dollar was unaccounted for.

This is when I really learnt how to budget, and I think it's where a lot of my drive comes from. I know what it's like to have nice things, and I know what it's like to go without. I know how easily your situation can change. I knew then and I know now what I want my life to be like. What I want my children's lives to be like. And I also know that sometimes, no matter how hard you try, things don't work out.

I know what it's like to have nice things, and I know what it's like to go without. I know how easily your situation can change. I knew then and I know now what I want my life to be like. What I want my children's lives to be like. And I also know that sometimes, no matter how hard you try, things don't work out.

Back to secondhand shopping: in my mind, I had connected visiting op-shops with having no money. With being in a tight spot. When I first left home, had next to no money and was living in overdraft, I should have been shopping at op-shops. Did I? No. I bought EVERYTHING brand-new. I would rather borrow money than step foot in an op-shop. I didn't connect safeguarding money with being thrifty. I saw buying new as being successful and buying secondhand as failing.

Do I still think that? No. No way.

The funniest thing changed my mind. I was around at a friend's house one day and noticed a crystal decanter on the bench. I was drawn in like a magpie and asked my friend where she got it. 'I didn't,' she said. 'Mum got it from an op-shop.'

An op-shop! I was amazed.

She laughed. 'Why is that surprising to you?'

I stopped to think. I realised there must be a lot of decanters in op-shops. They've gone somewhat out of fashion, so older generations must clear them out and donate them.

I was conflicted. I *liked* decanters. I *wanted* a decanter. A brand-new one would be around $200. Could I justify that? Should I go to an op-shop? Just one? To have a look?

I asked Kaitlyn to take me to our local op-shop – I couldn't go alone. And guess what.

I LEFT WITH FIVE BLOODY DECANTERS.

Enter the obsession. The awakening. The new me. OP-SHOPS ROCK!

That's what kicked off my obsession with decanters. I scoured op-shops near and far, finding all sorts of awesome decanters for $10 here and $5 there. Until, as you know, my wife told me I needed to stop, pointing out I had lost all control. She asked me to count them and I realised in a few short weeks I had amassed no fewer than 70 decanters. Whoops.

Decanters opened up the world of op-shopping for me, knocking down the wall I had built up. Now, looking around my home, I see a lot of my favourite items are secondhand, and they take pride of place. If I want something, I now first check op-shops or sites like Trade Me or Facebook Marketplace to see if I can find a bargain. Most of the time, I find what I want at a great price. Gone are the days of thinking it would all be garbage. Finding the hidden gems is half the fun – and I can proudly tell people I got something secondhand and watch their amazement.

Secondhand shopping can amp up your mindfulness and reduce the amount you are spending overall, you will be helping the environment, and you're most likely buying something that your neighbours don't have. There is no downside! Why not try it?

Share or pass along unused items

So often we have things that just sit there. We don't use them regularly or at all, and they just take up space. Sharing these things with those around us, as well as passing things along when we no longer need them, is such a great gift. Not only does it mean that there's less stuff in the world, but it also saves us money and gives us warm, fuzzy feelings!

We were lucky enough to be given a trampoline by someone a few blocks away. Friends helped us carry it over a few streets to our home. It looked hilarious, but it was also a powerful reminder about how awesome community is.

Reach out. Make those connections. Swap excess produce with your neighbours. Join or start a local book, toy or tool library. Check out 'buy nothing' or 'zero waste' groups on social media.

Community really is magic.

things to share or pass along within your community

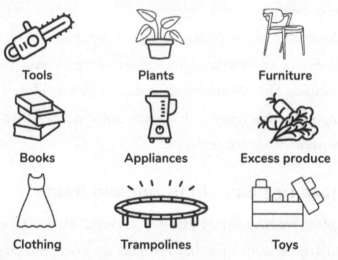

Tools   Plants   Furniture

Books   Appliances   Excess produce

Clothing   Trampolines   Toys

The classic money challenge

This is a story about a man who, in my humble opinion, completed one of the best money challenges of all time. You have probably heard of him. Back in 2005, Canadian blogger

Kyle MacDonald traded one humble red paperclip all the way up to a house in just fourteen online trades over one year.

Kyle traded:

1. one red paperclip for a fish-shaped pen
2. the pen for a hand-sculpted doorknob
3. the doorknob for a Coleman camp stove (with fuel)
4. the camp stove for a Honda generator
5. the generator for an 'instant party': an empty keg, an IOU for filling the keg with the beer of the bearer's choice, and a neon Budweiser sign
6. the 'instant party' for a Ski-Doo snowmobile
7. the snowmobile for a two-person trip to Yahk, British Columbia
8. the second spot on the Yahk trip for a box truck
9. the box truck for a recording contract with Metalworks in Mississauga, Ontario
10. the contract for a year's rent in Phoenix, Arizona
11. the year's rent in Phoenix for one afternoon with Alice Cooper
12. the afternoon with Alice Cooper for a KISS motorised snow globe
13. the snow globe for a role in the film *Donna on Demand*
14. the movie role for a two-storey farmhouse in Kipling, Saskatchewan.

This is some seriously impressive trading, and at a time when posting and sharing online was not nearly what it is today. Following Kyle's success, countless people (mostly YouTubers) have done the challenge with loads of different outcomes.

This is the kind of money challenge that doesn't require much to get going. You could start with a random low-value item from around the house (like a paperclip) or you could make or buy something. The only rule of the game is that everything has to be traded. You don't need to limit yourself to a timeframe – it's more about finding a good trade. If Kyle can do it online in 2005, you can do it now. Think of all the different places you could post to find trades – the world is your oyster!

Chapter 7

Buying a house

Now for the bit you have all been waiting for … buying a house! But not just buying a house – being able to own your house outright without a pesky mortgage. It is a long process, but one that is worth it in the end. And if you make some smart decisions with your money (and have a bit of luck!) you hopefully won't be lumped with a mortgage for the rest of your life either.

How Kaitlyn and I did it

Just after Kaitlyn and I got married in 2017, we looked over at each other one night and said, 'Now what?' We had to laugh at ourselves. Being Mr and Mrs Vanilla, we knew EXACTLY what we wanted: get married, have kids and live happily ever after. Picket fence and all. But how were we going to do this? We knew that we didn't want to raise kids in Auckland; it was just too expensive. But we did like the

Kāpiti Coast, near Wellington, which is where I grew up. So we set a plan. We gave ourselves two years (the time it would take Kaitlyn to finish her degree) to get rid of our debt and save up enough money to buy a house.

So that's exactly what we did. We saved our asses off and used all the methods I've talked about in this book.

When it came time to buy, we discovered that what we could afford was in a different reality from what we'd had in mind. First we found a company that prebuilt houses in a factory and trucked them to your section. It seemed a lot cheaper and quicker than building from scratch. I opted for a three-bedroom, two-bathroom house with all the toppings: a walk-in wardrobe, a butler's pantry ... the works. I thought we'd be able to make this dream a reality – I was dead set on it, actually. But when it came down to it, we didn't have enough saved and we weren't going to get as much from KiwiSaver as we had hoped. I do not take setbacks well. It took me a good month of—

'You better write "sulking" because that's what it was!' my wife just interjected.

Yes, it took me a good month of sulking to get over it.

Then we started looking for a house. We started at the top end of our budget and quickly realised that houses were selling at prices far higher than what they were advertised for. Again we had to reset our sights.

We moved down to Kāpiti and into a small room at my mum's place. We now also had a baby on the way and were starting to feel a bit desperate. Prices were continuing to rise and our money was not keeping up. It was now or never.

Luckily, we found a place that we really liked. It had two bedrooms, was about 80 square metres, and had its own back section. It needed a bit of renovation, but everything was cosmetic. Our max budget was $380,000. We had saved $20,000 in cash and the rest of our deposit would be covered by our KiwiSavers. Putting in an offer was really daunting. They say to offer whatever you feel comfortable with, but how does that help?! How do you know how much is the right amount to offer for a house? We really wanted the place, but we also didn't want to spend all our money. We knew we'd want to renovate it, so we would need money for that.

We put in an offer of $360,000.

A week later we were told our offer had been declined. Someone else's offer had been accepted. It sold for $370,000. We were gutted. We could have afforded it and we let it slip through our fingers.

We found another house. It already had an offer on it, but that person was pulling out because of money issues. It was a two-bedroom, 70-square-metre back unit. Cute, sunny, but a far cry from what I'd wanted to begin with.

We put in an offer of $380,000. Our max.

It was accepted. We had bought a house in the nick of time before our baby arrived. I cried, but not from happiness. I didn't love that house. I didn't want that house. It didn't make me feel happy. In hindsight, this was 100% buyer's remorse. And understandably so – it was the biggest purchase of my life and I didn't even like it that much. Thankfully the feeling didn't last too long.

> **66**
>
> **We had bought a house in the nick of time before our baby arrived. I cried, but not from happiness. I didn't love that house. I didn't want that house. It didn't make me feel happy. In hindsight, this was 100% buyer's remorse.**
>
> **99**

Moving in was so much fun – we had all this space just for us! And the feeling of knowing we could do whatever we wanted to it was something that to this day makes me so happy.

We had that house for a year. We spent $8,000 renovating it – we painted, put in some new fixtures and tidied the place up – and it's where we had our first child. We grew to love the house. It was our haven, and I will always hold it so dear in my heart. We often reminisce about that home and how happy we were there.

But we soon realised that things were going to be a little too cosy if we were to have another kid. We started looking around just to see what we could afford. Almost like magic, this MASSIVE house popped up. It was a 240-square-metre, three-bedroom, two-bathroom house with a huge basement. It also had a big 800-square-metre section. And it was in our price range!

Everything became clear when we went to see it. The list of issues was a mile long: the basement leaked through the back wall, the roof was leaking, the kitchen was falling apart, the whole house stank and was filthy, one bedroom upstairs had no lining or flooring, the section was overgrown. There was at least $100,000 worth of work to get it back to its former glory.

And yet there was something about this house. We knew what it could become.

We put in an offer. They wanted over $500,000 for it. Not wanting to miss out again, we offered $530,000 on the condition of our house selling. It was accepted and we were so excited! We immediately listed our house for sale. We were hoping for $450,000 – we'd only had it a year after all, and we hadn't spent much on renovations.

Our mouths fell open when it sold ONE WEEK later for $504,000. That's $124,000 more than what we'd paid for it just a year before. Happy is an understatement. We'd be able to do a lot of the work on the new house straight away.

I will never forget the day we moved in. You know how I got buyer's remorse about the first place? Well, Kaitlyn and I both got it this time. Moving all our things into this filthy house with tons of issues was so overwhelming. What on earth had we done? Were we out of our minds?

We turned to focus on the first stage of renovation, and these feelings soon turned to excitement.

We only had about $35,000 to spend. If we wanted more money from the bank, we'd need more income. We came up with a win–win situation. We'd tackle the biggest issue first, and at the same time create a way to increase our income: we planned to convert the massive 100-square-metre ground floor into a garage and a studio flat that we could rent out.

Kaitlyn and I called in a team of builders and were just about to get started when Covid-19 hit. While we waited to move down alert levels, we stripped the house of its tons of wallpaper. It took weeks – I never want to do that job ever again!

At last the builders could go about the job downstairs. But, as with any renovation project, unexpected costs came up and money ran out fast. In the end, we had to get the team to stop when the project was about 80% complete. Kaitlyn and I chipped away at it ourselves over the next few months, bringing in tradies for short bursts when we could afford it.

Finally the studio was finished and we advertised it. An awesome young couple moved in and we gave them a decent price. (We didn't want to be those people who charge an arm and a leg just because we can. That's never been our aim.) At last the bank would give us more money!

We continued renovating the rest of the house – ghastly carpet, wallpaper and all. We painted the whole house and did some landscaping, I got my brother to show me how to hang GIB, and we did a whole heap of demolition. It took longer than it would've if we'd hired tradies, but we saved heaps and could splash out on new flooring for the entire house, which was such a treat. The kitchen looked a million bucks, and the laundry had a nice bench and massive tub. It was a proper house. It was awesome.

Our second baby came along as we were finishing up the renovations; Kaitlyn was tiling the kitchen the day she went into labour!

Around this time, our first child was becoming more adventurous. She wanted to play outside and explore, but the section was incredibly steep – something we hadn't really thought out. We were also realising just how much our house had gone up in value. Some real estate agents predicted around $750,000 – we hadn't even had the house for a year! We did some thinking and decided it might be best to find a place where our kids could safely play outside. We looked and looked, but we couldn't find anything.

The problem was that while our house had gone up in value, so had everything else in the area. When you're buying and selling in the same market, you're likely to get something similar to what you already have, unless you are spending a lot more money than what you are selling for. Kaitlyn and I didn't want to do that – we couldn't afford to. I was the only one earning at the time, so we needed our mortgage to stay about the same.

When our second baby was 11 days old, an empty section about 20 minutes' drive away came up for sale. It was cheap, huge and by the beach – Kaitlyn's dream. We went and had a look. There were a few issues with retaining walls around the perimeter that would need to be sorted, but we realised that we could have the same mortgage and a property that ticked all our boxes. It was all we'd ever dreamt of, and we never thought we would be able to have it so soon.

So we put in an offer. They wanted $340,000, but we knew there would be plenty of interest. We were ready to jump on it. We offered $380,000 on the condition of our house sale. It seemed crazy to us that in just two years we'd gone from paying that for a house to paying that for a section. But, hey, that was the market at that time.

The offer was accepted. We listed our house. Three weeks later it sold.

For $835,000.

That's $305,000 more than we had bought it for. In 11 months.

Like I said, the market was wild.

In two years, we'd gone from having $20,000 to roughly $360,000. The biggest lesson I learnt was: the day we bought our first house, the day I cried saying I hated it, was the day we made the best decision we have ever made. We were on the property ladder. We had gone with the market instead of watching everything get more and more expensive without us.

In two years, we'd gone from having $20,000 to roughly $360,000. The biggest lesson I learnt was: the day we bought our first house, the day I cried saying I hated it, was the day we made the best decision we have ever made.

However, while this was a good gain over two years, we were still buying and selling in the same market. All the numbers were getting bigger, so what we could actually get for our money hadn't changed in a major way. We'd bought a section for $380,000 that was mostly mortgage-free ... but we still had to build a house. And with building costs majorly rising, we would not be seeing a smaller mortgage any time soon.

And so came the journey of building a house.

At the outset we wanted a mortgage that was smaller or about the same. We went with a building company that listed their prices and were upfront about all the costs. We knew what we were getting into – or so we thought. Kaitlyn wanted to build a house that was just what we needed and no more. I wanted to build a house that was way beyond what we needed. I wanted a spare bedroom, walk-in wardrobe and second lounge. After a lot of debate, we met in the middle. We knew this meant our mortgage was unlikely to be smaller, but we thought it'd end up in the same ballpark. We picked a house and worked with the building company to tweak it and make it our own. It was going to cost $340,000 all up. Not a bad price, we thought.

Before any building could take place, we knew we would need to put in three retaining walls: one along the driveway; one on the opposite side of the driveway that would hold up the neighbour's property, which was higher than ours; and one at the back of the section to replace a wall that was falling down. Our builders asked if we would like them to do the job for us – they quoted around $65,000. With hindsight we should have said yes, but you know where this is going. We did not.

Six months down the track, we are living in a tiny 40-square-metre house and we've made next to no progress on our new house, a build we'd hoped would take us nine months total. The contractor we hired to put in the retaining walls, in short, did not (revisit Chapter 3 if you need a refresher on that nightmare) and we were facing the exact same hurdle we'd started out with. Unfortunately, by this time the price of building the house had gone up, and our building company was no longer available to do the retaining work themselves. We had to find a new contractor. We went with someone recommended by the building company who quoted us $65,000 for the three walls. They couldn't start until March, but about eight weeks after that they'd finished the job.

It had taken 18 months, but we were at last ready to start building!

As you can imagine, this whole process was extremely trying. It's one of the hardest things Kaitlyn and I have ever done (aside from having kids) and definitely the most frustrating. For months, we had been seeing absolutely no progress and yet were paying money left, right and centre. There were specialist fees, we were paying a mortgage, rent and our usual day-to-day costs, and we had to pay big chunks towards deposits for the house and the retaining walls.

We had a lot of bad days where we questioned if any of it was worth it. If we'd looked at the situation with a purely financial mind, it probably wasn't. But the problem with building a house is it is not just a financial decision – it's an emotional one. When you're dealing with such strong emotions and money, it's hard to make sensible decisions.

After we parted ways with the first contractor and things seemed really bleak, we considered pulling the plug. We could have sold the section and just bought a house. But we knew that if we did that, we would lose even more money and we'd probably only be able to afford a house that was worse than the one we had sold.

Giving up was not an option.

reminder:

go easy on yourself for your past money mistakes. you were only doing your best with the knowledge and resources you had at the time.

When we finally got to the actual building of the house, things started to go pretty quickly. It was amazing to see progress every week! We had loads of decisions to make, and because of the issues we'd had I'd taken an all-in approach. I went a little overboard. I figured that we had already gone this far, and prices had risen so much, that we might as well spend that bit extra and get exactly what we wanted. After all, it's not every day you build a house.

I am very, very happy with our wonderful house and I wouldn't change anything about it, but we do now have a much larger mortgage than we planned – something we said we wouldn't fall into. Yes, there were things that we couldn't see coming, and we were messed around, but we did also go a bit over the top. All in all, the house alone ended up costing $476,000. That's $136,000 more than what we had first accepted. On top of that was the amount we ended up paying for the retaining wall issues, and then all the other fees and bits and bobs like landscaping that come with building a house. And *then*, right at the end, there were all the expenses you don't think about that pop out of nowhere!

the final expenses for our new-build home

Code of compliance   Finishing the deck   Towel rails

Finishing retaining   Curtains in the   Trees from
wall #4   living areas   Marketplace

Deck stain   Driveway chip   Celebrations!

I kept a spreadsheet to track all our expenses so I know exactly how much it all cost us, but I won't embarrass myself by telling you. Too much.

Now the plan is: hunker down, pay off the mortgage.

There are silver linings to all this. We now have a beautiful house we love with a big section in a great area. Luckily for us, the new-build house market hasn't slumped, while all around us the rest of the housing market has. We actually have quite good equity in our home, should we need or want to use it, despite the equally large mortgage.

So what's the point of this big story?

1. Get on the property ladder – it doesn't really matter what you buy, just buy something. (Okay, make sure a builder checks it out first.)
2. Look into money-saving ways to renovate, like DIY.
3. Be creative. Think outside the box. And be prepared for the plan to change – multiple times.

Okay. So you've got a budget, a plan and some tricks up your sleeve, and you are ready to buy that damn house. Yippee! Let's suss out the details.

Step 1: How much can you afford?

It's really easy to figure this out. All you need to do is google a mortgage calculator. Find a 'How much can I borrow?' tool, and enter in your deposit and income details. Find a calculator that will factor in any dependants (kids) and loans, as this is what a real bank will do when you apply.

Your deposit might be made up of some combination of the following:

- savings
- gifted money (any cash you may have got from relatives – you lucky duck, if that's you!)
- KiwiSaver (minus the $1,000 government kick-start amount – if you received this, it must stay in the account)
- KiwiSaver First Home Grant (check if you're eligible)
- Kāinga Ora First Home Partner (again, check if you're eligible, but could be up to $200,000).

And your income might be:

- regular wages or salary (chat with your mortgage broker if you haven't been in your current role for

very long or you're on a fixed-term contract – it's
certainly not a deal breaker, but be aware that banks
like to see stability before they'll lend to you)

- regular income from IRD (for example, Best Start
  payments or Working for Families Tax Credits)
- self-employed income (again, a mortgage broker can
  help if this is you, but know you'll need good records
  over at least two years for most banks – just a few
  more hoops with this one!).

(If any of the different things I listed above are new to
you, flick to the glossary on pages 219–226 for a longer
explanation.)

Online calculators often have an option to 'apply' for
a mortgage. You can try this, but my advice is to talk to a
mortgage broker. Mortgage brokers are like little mortgage
angels who take away your problems and bring you solutions.
They know all the tricks of the trade and can get you a great
deal on a mortgage. They may even be able to help you get
approved if you have tricky circumstances. Best of all, they
are free!

Once you know how much you can borrow, it's over to
the bank or mortgage broker to get a 'preapproval', which
means the bank will let you know how much they are willing
to lend you on top of your deposit. You will now know the
maximum you can spend on a house at this time.

what are mortgage brokers?

Act as the middle person between the borrower (you) and the lender (usually the bank)

Can negotiate on your behalf

They often have relationships with multiple lenders and access to the interest rates they offer

Regulated by the Financial Markets Authority (in NZ)

Will act in your best interest, based on your personal financial situation and goals

Usually offer services free of charge to the borrower because they get paid a commission from the lender

Can come up with out-of-box solutions for borrowing if your circumstances don't fit in the standard mould

Can help out with paperwork and understanding complex jargon

Step 2: Your options

Once you know what you can afford, you might find that reality hits home. You may not be able to afford the kind of place you wanted, but you may also be pleasantly surprised. Whatever the outcome, I would advise you to avoid looking at the top end of your budget. The advertised price on a house is rarely the amount it sells for. Most houses will go for a good deal more. Some houses won't, of course, and some might even go for lower than their advertised price, but at the time of writing there are more people who want houses in New Zealand than there are houses. Demand is outstripping supply. Which means that, nine times out of ten, you will need to stump up more cash. So it's best to have some wiggle room by finding something on the lower end of your price range.

What makes a good first buy and what makes a bad first buy? Most houses in New Zealand would be classed as a good buy. The only thing to really look out for is the state of a house's foundations, frame and roof. If there aren't any structural flaws, then the house has good 'bones'. You can feel relatively confident that it's not going to suddenly fall to pieces.

First-home buyers should avoid houses that have big, costly fixes. Your first home needs to be something safe to live in that you can look after yourself. If you happen to be a builder and you can handle expensive structural repairs, then great. But, for most of us, sticking to solid houses is a wise choice. To make sure you are not getting a lemon, get a builder to do an inspection before you put an offer on a house, or have a builder's inspection as one of the conditions of your offer.

It's also important not to confuse the soundness of a house with cosmetics (the way it looks). A shitty old kitchen, terrible colour choices or peeling wallpaper is fine! In fact, the more of it, the better. It may put some other buyers off and help keep the price down. You can easily change these later. They won't cost too much to update and doing so can add real value and buyer appeal to the house. Get the cheapest, ugliest house you can that has solid bones. This is the kind of house that will make you money.

It's also important not to confuse the soundness of a house with cosmetics (the way it looks). A shitty old kitchen, terrible colour choices or peeling wallpaper is fine! In fact, the more of it, the better. It may put some buyers off and help keep the price down.

When looking at your options, make sure that you view plenty of properties. Don't make the mistake of writing somewhere off when you've only seen it online. If it's in your budget and in the right location, definitely go and see it in person. I've seen plenty of houses I've liked online only to turn up and feel catfished, but there have been just as many I wasn't sure about online that blew me away in person. It's like Tinder for houses, really – you don't know what they are truly like till you meet 'em.

Lots of first-home buyers (myself included) make the mistake of thinking they need to fall in love with the first house they buy. This makes sense. It's the most money you have ever spent, it's a goal you've worked towards for what feels like a lifetime, and it's a huge decision. But remember that your first home is highly unlikely to be your 'forever' home. You really don't have to be head over heels in love. Think about it like you might a first job. You probably won't love it. You might not even like it very much. But it's a step towards what you really want. And, once you have taken that crucial step and got that first job or first house, your future really opens up. It's like having sex for the first time: there's a lot of emotions and stress and build-up, and it's unlikely that you enjoy it, but once it's done, it's done – time to learn and move on to bigger and better things. Good metaphor, right?

So, in short, just buy a house. But not a dud one.

Step 3: Buying the house

Okay, so you have the cash and you've picked the house you want. Now what? Make an offer!

Make sure you understand the house's real value versus what it's listed for. How much you should offer comes down to this: if you were to make an offer that got rejected, would you feel disappointed? Would you know you could have offered more to be the one who got it? If so, your offer is not high enough. Offer what you feel it is worth and what you can afford. Lay all your cards on the table and put your best offer forward. There is no point in trying to play the game. If you make a low offer to try to get a cheeky bargain, most of the time you will miss out. Trust me. Been there, done that, and cried about it.

When you make an offer, you will hear about 'conditions'. Conditions are things that need to be met from your end to warrant the offer being 'unconditional', meaning that no matter what you will pay that price for the house.

You'll need to have a lawyer for this part. Before you make an offer, find a local lawyer who deals with house purchases and talk to them about what conditions you should include. (You'll need this lawyer again later down the track when confirming the house purchase.) Remember that while conditions keep you safe, they also slow down the purchase of a house. Sellers tend to go for offers with fewer or no conditions, because every condition that needs to be met is a barrier to getting the house sold. The seller will look for the best offer (dollar-wise) with the fewest conditions. It's a tricky thing to weigh up, but that is what conversations with your lawyer are for!

Typical conditions include the following.

- **Certificate of title**
  This allows for your lawyer to do a search of the property to check its title and make sure you are buying the right place! These are normally under $10.
- **Builder's report**
  You can add this in if you would like to get a builder to check that everything in the house is okay before

you buy. It can be good to get a builder's report *after* your offer has been accepted, rather than potentially wasting money on a report beforehand when you might not even put an offer in. But remember: the more conditions you have, the more likely the seller will go with someone else's offer. Weigh it up. The cost of a builder's report depends on who you get, but it's normally around $500 to $600.

- **Finance**

  This condition is to make sure the bank is happy to lend you the money you need to buy the house. Even if you have preapproved finance, it's good to have this condition as banks like to make sure they are not lending too much for a house worth much less. They will require a valuation to be done on the house. A valuation normally costs around $700.

- **LIM report**

  A Land Information Memorandum (LIM) report is a summary of information that the district council holds on a property. When you apply for a LIM, the council will prepare a report that includes some or all of the following property information:

  - special land features or characteristics (including potential erosion, slippage or subsidence)
  - private and public storm water and sewerage drains

- any rates that may be owing in relation to the land
- information concerning building, plumbing
  or drainage, and resource planning consents
  (including notice, order or requisition affecting the
  land or any building)
- special conditions, including New Zealand
  Historic Places Trust listings
- any information that has been notified to the
  council by any statutory organisation in terms of
  any other act
- network utility in relation to the Building Act
  1991 or 2004.

It is not necessary to get a LIM report, and some
houses for sale will have them available so there is no
need to order your own. Talk to your lawyer about
the necessity of getting one. A LIM report will cost
around $500.

There are other conditions you can add in – the best thing
to do is talk to your lawyer. There may be specific things you
want to be sure of before you go unconditional on a house.

Each condition will have a time attached to it, meaning
the condition will need to be met by the time specified.
Make sure you give yourself enough time with each one –
talk to your lawyer and mortgage broker to know how long
you will need.

When you have decided on your conditions and made your offer, the real estate agent will let you know if the offer has been accepted. This usually takes a few days, depending on if there is a deadline or not. Don't be surprised if your offer is not accepted. It's not very common for your first, second or even third offer to be accepted, especially if there's a lot of competition. Don't get disheartened though – keep looking and trying. Sometimes the seller will come back with a counteroffer, which basically means they give you a new price and ask that you offer that much. It's all part of the negotiations. If you have already gone in with your best offer, stick to your guns. There is no point going above that figure if you can't afford it.

If your offer is accepted, it's basically a countdown to the unconditional date: the day you have agreed to buy the house no matter what. To get there, you'll need to tick all your conditions off and let the seller know (your lawyer will do this). If you don't quite manage to get everything done in time, you can ask for an extension – a few days to be added on to your unconditional date. It's best to avoid this if you can, even just for the hassle, and it's not guaranteed your request will be accepted. The seller has every right to refuse and accept someone else's offer. That's how we bought our first house! We were that second offer.

After all your conditions have been met and your offer becomes unconditional, you will pay your deposit to the seller's lawyer. They will hold it in a trust until the settlement day. Settlement day is the day after unconditional day (which you and the seller will have agreed on), and it's the day you take full ownership of your new house. You and your bank will have organised to have the full amount for the house, minus the deposit, paid into the seller's account. Then you can collect the keys and move in! Woohoo!

buy a house!

Make your best offer

Understand and meet your conditions

Negotiate if needed

Move in on settlement day

Step 4: Mortgage repayments

Buying a house is one thing, but paying a mortgage on it is another! If you have never paid a mortgage before, the idea might seem daunting, but keep in mind that it often costs less than rent, because you are contributing towards something you own. When you start out with a mortgage, the longest term you can have it for is 30 years. This means that the sum of money you borrow from day one will be paid off in 30 years if you meet all your repayments. It can be longer if you end up 'topping up' your mortgage (borrowing more) later down the track. I'm sure the prospect of paying off a mortgage over 30 years seems like a long time. And it is! So why not try to get there a bit faster?

Over time, interest rates for home loans can fluctuate a lot. There are a few things you can do to pay off your loan faster and play it safe with interest. One way is to split your mortgage: have some of it, perhaps half, on a fixed rate for a short amount of time, say six months or a year (these timeframes usually have the lowest rates because there is less risk to the banks that rates will change significantly); then fix the other half of your mortgage for longer, two or more years. This way, only half of your mortgage is coming up for a fixed-term change at a time. If interest rates rise suddenly, you will still have one half of your mortgage at an older (presumably lower) rate, and your budget won't take a massive hit if your repayments increase. If interest rates are lower when you refix part of your mortgage, the bank will let you repay a lower amount. If this happens to you, it's wise not to lower your repayments – keep them the same or even raise them if you can afford to. You will be working towards your home loan being paid off even faster.

As a default, when you start paying your mortgage off you will be paying the minimum repayment – this is the minimum amount you can pay in order to pay off the mortgage in the loan timeframe. Paying more than the minimum will mean you end up paying off your loan faster (and you will pay less interest on it!). There is a maximum the bank will let you pay off as well.

You might remember that in Chapter 4 I talked about how money in your long-term savings account can go towards paying off your mortgage even faster. Each time your mortgage comes up to be refixed, you have the opportunity to pay a lump sum on it without being penalised. This means that, for a brief period of time (talk to your bank about the dates), even just one day, you can have a 'floating' mortgage and can pay as much as you like without paying breakage fees. (The bank charges breakage fees when you pay a chunk of your mortgage off or cancel a fixed-term rate early. This charge makes up for the money they would have made off you if you had continued at the fixed rate.)

Is it smart to pay off a mortgage quicker? Yes, as outlined in Chapter 4, it is much better for you and your finances if you put your money towards paying off your mortgage faster rather than keeping it in a savings account. Savings accounts will always earn much less interest than will be added to your mortgage. Say you had a $500,000 mortgage over 30 years. You would pay the bank $359,347 in interest over that time (based on an interest rate of 4%). But, if you paid off chunks and kept your repayments above the minimum so that your mortgage was paid off in 20 years, you would pay the bank $227,176 in interest. That's $132,171 less! Hello, new Tesla?!

At the end of the day, do your best. You won't be able to always pay off chunks or keep your repayments high – life happens! Just stick to the principles and you will be surprised at how well you can do.

It's a good idea to talk to a mortgage broker about all this and what is right for you. I've described the method that works for me, but you may need something different. The important thing to take from all this is to realise that you do not have to have a mortgage for 30-plus years. You can set goals to pay it off sooner, and there are ways to do it. Do you remember when I talked about offsetting? Our mortgage broker suggested that, and now some of our mortgage is connected to our everyday accounts so that when we have money in there it counts against the money we owe and we don't pay interest on that part of the loan. It's truly amazing the number of crafty things that someone in the know can rustle up!

Chapter 8

When things don't go to plan

Things don't always go the way we'd like. And don't we know it! How bloody good would it be if everything always worked out for the best? The sun would always shine, dinner plans would never be cancelled, and we would pay off all our debts in two easy payments. Yeah, right.

This is not how the world works. In this world, we have to contend with a multitude of different factors that can ruin our plans. And, unfortunately, sometimes we have to face them all at once.

Recession

What is a recession? Why is everyone talking about it? What does it mean?!

If a country is going through a recession, this simply means that it is making less money than it did in the few months prior. A bit more technically, a recession is an economic downturn characterised by a significant decline in economic activity over a sustained period. It is typically marked by a decrease in gross domestic product (GDP), which is the value of all goods and services produced within a country.

A country in a recession acts like an individual does when faced with less money to spend: it cuts back costs and is a bit more risk averse when looking at investments. In the economy, business profits might decline, unemployment rates might increase, consumer spending might go down, and there will be a slowdown in overall economic growth.

Lots of different things can cause a recession, but I won't bore you by overexplaining all the complexities. (To be honest, I'm not even sure I understand all of it.) What I will talk about is how to prepare for a recession, the impact it will have on you, and what to do when you are in one.

There are three key impacts a recession is likely to have on you: the cost of living will likely be high, income will likely be lower than it needs to be, and jobs will be harder to come by. While all this does sound scary, there is no need for panic. If you follow some simple preparation steps, then you will hopefully be spared any negative impacts.

Recessions can last a few months or even a few years. While they can be unpredictable, it's certain that having savings will help. The cost of borrowing money in a slow economy is higher, therefore you want to pay down as much debt as possible. Have an emergency fund available if you can so you don't need to borrow for unforeseen situations.

You could try to secure a permanent job if you don't already have one to give yourself more job security. If you don't have a secure job, consider purchasing income insurance.

Stay steady with your investments. In an economic downturn, your investments will likely lose value. Don't panic and sell. The market will go back up and your investments will be worth the same or more again. Remember, the moment you sell an investment for less than you bought it for is the moment you have made a loss. No sale = no loss.

There is one pretty good silver lining to a recession: after high costs of living, leading to a recession, costs tend to drop. Demand for products goes down because people are spending less, so businesses lower the cost of items to drive sales back up. Fortunately, this tends to be the case with mortgage rates. So a recession can be a great time to buy a house. Prices may be lower because sellers are more motivated and mortgage rates may be lower too.

Inflation

Inflation measures how the price of goods and services goes up over time. Inflation can make it harder to afford things because the same stuff tends to cost more.

At the time of writing, wages in New Zealand are not, on average, keeping up with inflation. This means that living has become rather expensive for many people. One of the biggest drivers of inflation is supply not keeping up with demand, and during the Covid-19 pandemic supply dropped dramatically with little warning while demand kept growing. Global supply chains were heavily disrupted by lockdowns – something particularly evident in countries like China, where lockdowns pretty much halted the manufacturing of many materials and products that are exported globally. This affected everything from the automotive industry and electronics to clothing and furniture. Supply was also affected by widespread labour shortages. Job losses and illness further reduced the availability of goods and services – there just weren't enough people working. These shortages pushed up prices significantly.

At the same time as supply was severely reduced, demand grew. Many governments around the world provided stimulus packages – economic policies and actions designed to cushion the blow for people and businesses while stabilising the economy. The New Zealand government's stimulus package covered wage subsidies, health, increased benefits and tax relief for businesses. They paid for this by 'printing money' – money was created by the Reserve Bank and used to buy government bonds from banks and large corporations.

Some argue that this is the cause of the inflation we're experiencing today, but there is evidence to suggest that government spending during Covid-19 is not correlated with current inflation. Countries that didn't provide stimulus packages are also seeing high rates of inflation. Sweden, for example, didn't have a public health response to Covid-19, but at the time of writing their inflation rate is 10.6% – far higher than New Zealand's 6.7%.

After the 2007–2008 global financial crisis, both wages and inflation were around 1.5%, meaning products and services were relatively affordable. Everything changed when Covid-19 hit, and since then inflation has been rising far faster than wages can keep up. Other recent events contributing to rising inflation include Russia's invasion of Ukraine and Cyclone Gabrielle.

Inflation is a sign of a healthy economy – when it's low, predictable and stable. But when it's rapid and unforeseen it can have harmful consequences, like the cost-of-living crisis. The main way to lessen the effects of the cost-of-living crisis is to reduce inflation, which is why the Reserve Bank has a target inflation rate of 1% to 3%.

There are many ways decision-makers try to reduce inflation; different political parties have different ideas about what will be most effective. The Reserve Bank may try to reduce the rate of inflation by increasing the official cash rate (OCR), which means that the Reserve Bank charges banks more to borrow money. They do this in an effort to curb spending and reduce the demand that can contribute to inflation. The unpleasant outcome of this is that the cost is passed on to bank customers, who will have to pay higher interest rates on things like mortgages. Consumers will then have less money to spend, meaning demand will drop and so too should inflation.

Global events can have a significant impact on inflation, which individual governments often have little control over. They might implement policies to address inflation and the cost-of-living crisis, but there is debate about whether these policies provide effective solutions or make the problem worse. Some believe that the government should not intervene, and instead leave it solely to the Reserve Bank.

you can't budget your way out of a cost-of-living crisis.

inflation is a global phenomenon that ebbs and flows over time.

having financial-literacy skills like budgeting can make it easier to cope.

Negative equity

Equity is the difference between what you owe on a home versus what it could reasonably sell for. Negative equity is when your house is worth less than what you owe on it, meaning if you were to sell it, you would owe the bank money. This means no getting back your deposit or any gains you might have hoped to earn on the property while you owned it.

At the onset of the Covid-19 pandemic, a lot of people found themselves in a housing market where the prices and demand were high, and the cost of borrowing was low. Fast-forward a year or so and the market took a drastic downturn – house prices fell and the cost of borrowing soared. Many people found themselves suddenly in negative equity.

Negative equity is worrying for people who are struggling to keep up with mortgage payments, especially when interest rates rise. If someone cannot meet their minimum payments and they are forced to sell their home, they may be left with a mortgage to a bank and no house to show for it. Others who hoped to move may be unable to unless they are prepared to lose money and effectively start again.

So it's fair to say that being in negative equity is not fun. It can't really be avoided altogether (unless you don't purchase a house, which is no fun either), but you can minimise the effects by spending less than you have available. This way, you'll have more of a buffer and less of a mortgage. Easier said than done, right?

If you find yourself in negative equity, do your best to ride out the economic wave and wait for your house to once again be worth more than you owe. If you're struggling to meet your payments, talk to a mortgage broker to make sure you are getting the best rates possible. You could consider paying interest only until you can afford to start paying the principal again.

Job loss

Who else hears the term 'restructuring' and gets the chills? It is hands-down a fancy way of saying, 'Some of you are losing your jobs.' The only saving grace in these situations is that they normally drag it out for a long time, giving you more time to find a new job.

Finding a new job in the face of a job loss is hard. Hard because it puts a big strain on your mood, finances and relationships, but hard too because you are now in a situation you don't want to be in – the desperate jobseeker. No one wants to be that guy. It can feel like employers smell you a mile away, and you know they know you will accept any offer to be employed again as quickly as possible. Many of us have been or will be there at some point, but knowing that doesn't do much to soften the blow: job hunting while facing a job loss is no fun.

So what can you do to protect yourself? Is there any way to avoid being desperate Dave sending out 100 job applications a night? (It is a numbers game at the end of the day though, Dave, so keep those applications up!)

Two things: income protection and an emergency fund.

Yes, I know – again with the emergency fund. When I first mentioned emergency funds in Chapter 1, I suggested tucking away what you could to cover unexpected bills. Now I want to talk about the real power of an emergency fund. Imagine having two to three months to find a new job rather than two to three weeks. How much more secure would you feel?

Aim to have two to three months of your expenses in an emergency fund to ensure you can cover your bum when shit hits the fan. And I know saving up this much is a hard thing to manage – heck, I haven't got there yet! But it's something to aim for. Imagine how freeing it'll feel once you get there.

If you team up a well-stocked emergency fund with income protection (insurance), the real magic starts to happen. Depending on the kind you opt for, you can purchase income insurance that will pay you up to your full salary for a good few years! Then if you lose your job or something happens to you that means you can't work for a period of time, you are covered. Often with these insurances, the longer the waiting period (time from losing your income to receiving your payout), the lower the premium.

So that's the ultimate safety net: enough savings in your emergency fund to cover the waiting period, plus income insurance with a lower premium – you'll be worry-free for years with no job!

Plan A to plan Z

There's a pretty simple common theme in this chapter when it comes down to it: plan ahead, save a good emergency fund, and plan ahead. Oh, did I mention planning ahead? Have a plan A, B, C ... you get it, right?

Chapter 9

Financial freedom

Goal setting

Back in Chapter 1, I briefly mentioned the idea of setting financial goals. Now is the time to do it. Your goals will drive you forward and help you understand what your next steps should be. As I write this, the average house price in New Zealand is sitting around $880,000. My bet is that getting onto the property ladder is the biggest goal for a lot of you, and I wouldn't be surprised if that goal feels unattainable.

It's hard, yes. But it is not impossible.

Think about your goals as a list. Start with the smallest one and end with the largest. Some smart people will probably tell you that achieving the small goals first and getting some quick wins is more psychologically fulfilling or some crap. I'm mainly interested in you getting rid of your debts and achieving your smaller goals before you focus on your main goal. This way, you can give all possible funds and attention to that one goal, and you'll have fewer distractions.

Your list of goals might look something like this:

1. Pay off Afterpay.
2. Pay Joe back.
3. Buy a new phone.
4. Buy a house.

Yeah, I know – that went to 100 real quick. But you get my drift. So now write your own list down.

My financial goals

1.

2.

3.

4.

5.

6.

Well done for getting those down. If you haven't just yet, have a think about them over the next few weeks. If you have a partner, talk to them. You need to be in lockstep when it comes to money. If you aren't, have the hard discussions. Money troubles are one of the main reasons for divorce. I don't say this to scare you, just to be realistic.

how to be on the same page as your partner about money

1 Start the conversation, e.g. 'I've been feeling stressed about our finances lately. Can we talk about it tonight?'

2 Sit down together to go through your bank statements and write a budget.

3 Allocate money for each of you to spend on whatever you like.

4 Write down your shared goals to find common ground.

5 Write down the steps you both need to take to stick to your budget and achieve your goals.

6 Have regular financial check-ins and celebrate together as you achieve your goals.

Make sure you have open and honest discussions with your partner about your financial goals and your budget. Talk about what you both want and how you plan on getting there. You may think that you're working towards the same things, but until you've had the conversation you don't know.

One of you might be planning to start saving, investing and cutting down, while the other may be happy coasting and thinking everything is fine. Get on the same page. And go see a financial advisor if you need to, so an unbiased person can look at your finances and goals and give you an objective path forward.

Retirement

Even if retirement is many, many years away for you yet, it's worth thinking seriously about it now. Retirement is ultimately the end goal of financial freedom – it's the reason you set your goals.

If you are young, you own a house, you're paying off a mortgage and you're contributing to your KiwiSaver, chances are you will be feeling pretty darn good about retirement. I mean, hell, I am. But you need – I need – to be realistic. Life happens, and things change. We do not know what the future will bring.

Remember at the end of the last chapter when I told you to have a plan? Yeah, I'm going to do that again. Make three plans for retirement: the ideal, the backup and the fallback.

If all goes according to plan, you will have a mortgage-free house, savings, KiwiSaver, a government pension and investments. That's plan A.

What happens if some of those things turn out not to be there? Plan B.

What happens if most of those things aren't there? Plan C.

At the time of writing, the retirement age in New Zealand is 65. Let's say you retire then and live until 95. That's 30 years of retirement, which also happens to be the length of a full mortgage. How much money will you need for that time?

Crack out the calculator. Figure out how much you will need to live on each year – $30,000 or $40,000 might be a good place to start (without costs like a mortgage and depending on your circumstances). Don't forget to account for inflation – things will always cost more in the future. Once you've worked out your yearly budget, times that by 30.

Now figure out how much you're on track to have by 65. Guess your future salary and the amount you will be contributing to KiwiSaver. There are online calculators for this too.

Do these calculations put things into perspective?

Think realistically. Don't tell yourself everything will be rosy and you will have life 'sorted out' by then. If you can be realistic, you're more likely to prepare and accept that things may not go as planned.

Consider what it would be like to continue to work. Not full-time and not necessarily in your current career, but a nice part-time job that pays for things like your groceries and petrol. Not only will working keep you active in retirement, it will also take the pressure off your finances.

Think realistically. Don't tell yourself everything will be rosy and you will have life 'sorted out' by then. If you can be realistic, you're more likely to prepare and accept that things may not go as planned.

Consider what it would be like to rent out a room in your home. This is a great way to earn extra income while also having company. One of the biggest challenges facing retirees is loneliness. If you can combat that while having an income stream, what is there to lose?

Be open to different ideas now so that you have an easier time accepting these realities if they present in the future.

Being wealthy

So how do you bring together everything you have learnt in this book? How do you make sure that you achieve financial freedom?

First things first: I am not a registered financial advisor (yet!) so please make sure you seek out advice from someone who is. They can give you feedback based on your individual circumstances and help you put the pieces of the puzzle together.

I can't tell you what to do or what not to do. I can only present you with what I have done, plan to do, and what I like the look of. So I'll tell you my financial goals and plans for at least the next ten years. Here goes!

As you now know, I have saved, worked and hustled to achieve the financial goals of home ownership and no consumer debt. I have had some good luck (and some bad luck) with the housing market, and I now have a fair amount of equity in my home. I also have a decent-sized mortgage.

I am a long way from financial freedom. A heck of a long way. My goal is to have a six-figure income without having to work, because I want to work when it suits me. When I feel like it. Not as dictated by my bills. Right now I am working to pay the bills and save towards my goals.

In the next ten years I'd like to pay off my mortgage and build up my investments. I want to create proper wealth.

The other day I heard a great comparison between being wealthy and being rich. A lot of people can be rich. Being rich means you have or earn a lot of money. Being wealthy doesn't necessarily mean that you are rich; it means that your income generated without you doing anything is covering your expenses. So, for example, if your passive income was

$1,000 a week and your expenses were $900 a week, I would consider that wealthy. Sure, that might not be rich, but if something happened and you couldn't work, your income generated without you doing anything – your wealth – would cover it. Less stress, more freedom.

So what is wealth? What is income generated without doing anything? How do you get a piece of that pie?

Investments. They are hands-down one of the best ways to generate wealth. Going to work each day will not bring you wealth. Getting a bigger paycheque will not bring you wealth. Sure, it might help you to start building wealth. But, until you have wealth, you have to work. And working is not wealth. It's paying the bills.

It's the classic saying: wealthy people don't work for money, their money works for them. Their investments earn money without them having to do anything. And, yes, you can start building that by doing everything I have talked about in this book. Budget well, cut down on expenses, earn more money and, most importantly, invest your money into assets that will bring you wealth: an income that is generated without you working for it.

The most common way a lot of people do this is by investing in shares. Shares pay out dividends if the business is achieving a profit, and if the business is doing well, and you have enough invested, you may start earning a good amount of income this way. It could take a while, however.

Investments like this are all about the long game: invest early and regularly, and use the power of time to let it grow.

Another common way of growing wealth is real estate. A lot of people buy investment properties for as little as possible and either 'flip' them and sell them on, or they rent them out. Real estate does involve a fair amount of risk (as does any investing), but it can usually have good returns. Kaitlyn and I have considered this option. When we rented out the bottom storey of our last house, it was a very positive investment for us. But we don't like the idea of building up an investment portfolio of houses that we rent out – it just doesn't sit with our values or interest us. I think that's important: you need to be interested in an investment. I want my money to go into something I genuinely care about. I could easily invest in oil companies, and I'm sure I'd make good money, but it's not just about money. I need to invest in something I believe in. If I don't feel good about the way I earn my money, I won't feel good about myself. And what is the point of that?

My main goal is to invest in businesses. I want to build a portfolio of businesses that will eventually run without me. In my mind, if I have to work at the business each day, it's a job. But, if I can set the business up or buy an established business, and then have little need for being hands-on – that's an investment. I am genuinely excited about the operations of a business. I have a lot of ideas that I want to turn into businesses, and I hope for them to be profitable, but I also see a lot of opportunities out there to purchase successful businesses. This way, I'll have a diversified portfolio with investments that are wide-ranging yet similar in practice – and I'll be sticking to my skillset as a business-minded person. You know in Chapter 4 when I talked about having a side hustle that capitalises on your natural skills and interests? Well, this would be an extension of that.

reminder:

budgeting is about so much more than the numbers.

it's about determining your goals and deciding where you want to be in life. it's about making purposeful, conscious steps in the right direction.

it's about figuring out what's important to you and what's not.

a good budget won't feel restrictive.

instead it will be freeing.

When it comes to you planning your financial freedom, I want you to take the messages in this book and apply them to your life. I want you to manage your money the best way you can and always be looking for ways to improve. When you plan your future and your goals, think about what you really want. It is only by knowing what you want and what you are aiming for that you will be able to figure out how to get there.

So meet with a financial advisor. Talk to your partner and your peers. Find the solutions that work best for you. There are so many different ways to manage your money and find financial freedom. Take the time to get it right. Remember this is a journey and you will make mistakes, and that is okay.

It's up to you

I hope that you have learnt something from this book. Something you can take and apply to your life to make a positive change. If you didn't learn anything, I hope you found some motivation. Motivation can be so very powerful. It can help you on your journey, reinvigorate your purpose and pull you out of a financial slump.

There will always be people in the world who are doing better than you, just as there will always be people who are doing worse. What I want you to focus on is your goals:

where you want to be and who you want to be. You won't get there with a positive mindset alone – it will take long, hard work – but there is a lot to be said for positivity. If you expect something to happen, believe that it can, and put in the hours, it's much more likely to happen. If you doubt yourself and think it can't happen, chances are it won't.

There will always be people in the world who are doing better than you, just as there will always be people who are doing worse. What I want you to focus on is your goals: where you want to be and who you want to be.

Don't be afraid of failure. Every time you fail, as much as it hurts, there is a lesson in there. You might not notice the lesson straight away – who likes the feeling of failing? – but a week, a month, a year later you will have that lightbulb moment where you realise how much you have learnt.

And never give up. If you give up on 'making it', whatever that looks like for you, that's when it slips out of reach. Pick yourself up, try again or do something different, but don't give up. Think of all the people before you who have gone through failure after failure to achieve the success they're looking for. It doesn't matter what age you are, what stage you're at in life, there is always a new day, another chance for you to turn things around.

And, if you need help to believe in yourself and think positively, then get help. See a counsellor or a therapist and talk about it. Build your self-confidence and positivity, and I promise you it will make a huge difference in your ability to achieve your goals.

You can do this. I am rooting for you. See you there.

Further reading

Budgeting and money management
- **Sorted** provide practical money support: sorted.org.nz
- **Money Talks** offer free support. Visit their website, moneytalks.co.nz, or give them a call on 0800 345 123.

Buying a house
- First Home Grant: https://kaingaora.govt.nz/home-ownership/first-home-grant
- Kāinga Ora First Home Partner: https://kaingaora.govt.nz/home-ownership/first-home-partner/

Books to keep you going on your journey to financial literacy
- *The Barefoot Investor*, Scott Pape
- *Rich Dad, Poor Dad*, Robert Kiyosaki
- *Girls That Invest*, Simran Kaur
- *The Total Money Makeover*, Dave Ramsey
- *Tales from a Financial Hot Mess*, Frances Cook

Glossary

asset

A useful or valuable thing (often cash or investments) or person.

bad debt

Normally defined as a debt that cannot be recovered, but in this book bad debt is unnecessary debt or debt that has a negative impact on your finances without good reason.

Best Start payments

For the first three years of your child's life, you are entitled to regular or lump-sum payments from IRD. For the first year, it's $60 a week guaranteed, then for the next two years it's based on your income with the max still being $60 a week.

breakage fee

A fee charged by a corporation when you end a contract early.

budget

An estimate of income and expenditure for a set period.

buyer appeal

If something has 'buyer appeal', it's something that buyers are attracted to purchase.

buyer's remorse

A feeling of regret experienced after making a purchase, typically a purchase regarded as unnecessary or extravagant.

compound interest

The interest on a loan or deposit that accrues on both the initial principal and the accumulated interest from previous periods.

condition

A requirement to be met before a sale can go through.

consolidation loan

A loan that brings all debts into one debt with one regular payment.

contents

Personal items you would want replaced if destroyed.

contractor

An employee who is not permanent or fixed-term is said to be a contractor.

counteroffer

An offer made in response to another.

debt

A sum of money that is owed or due.

dependant

A person who relies on another, especially a family member, for financial support.

deposit

A sum payable as a first instalment on the purchase of something or as a pledge for a contract, the balance being payable later.

excess

Part of an insurance claim to be paid by the insured.

extension (on an offer)

A new date that gives you more time than the previous date.

fixed bills

Bills that do not change.

fixed rate (mortgage)

A rate that is locked in for a period of time.

fixed-term contract

If you are working on a fixed-term contract, you have signed a contract to work in a job for a set amount of time (6, 12 or 18 months, for example).

freelance

A self-employed person who is hired to work for different companies on assignments.

fund

A group of businesses you buy shares in.

good debt

Debt for a financially sensible reason, like buying a house or higher education.

grant

A sum of money given by a government or other organisation for a particular purpose.

housing market

The supply and demand for houses.

inflation

A general increase in prices and fall in the purchasing value of money.

interest rate (home loan)

A rate that you pay on borrowing your mortgage. This is added to your principal payments.

interest rate (savings account)

The amount of money a bank or financial institution pays a depositor for holding their money. In a way, banks borrow money from their depositors by using the deposited funds to lend money to other customers.

investing

Putting money into financial schemes, shares, property or a commercial venture with the expectation of achieving a profit.

Kāinga Ora First Home Partner

This First Home Partner scheme run by Kāinga Ora is there to support you to get into your first home. If you can't get a big-enough loan from a bank to buy your first home, Kāinga Ora will contribute up to 25% of the purchase price or $200,000 (whichever is lower) to help you secure the home. In doing so, Kāinga Ora becomes a shared owner of your home. For example, you may have saved 10% of the purchase price of a home and a bank will loan you 75%. Kāinga Ora will contribute 15% to purchase the home with you in return for a 15% share of ownership. You'll need to have a minimum of 5% of the purchase price yourself, and you can purchase Kāinga Ora's percentage of the home back from them at the end of the agreement.

KiwiSaver

A voluntary savings scheme to help set you up for your retirement. You can make regular contributions from your pay or directly to your scheme provider.

KiwiSaver First Home Grant

A grant of up to $10,000 per person (max two) towards your first home. To be eligible, you need to have been contributing to your KiwiSaver for at least three years and fall under the income-cap threshold. How much you receive depends on things like your income and the type of home you want to buy.

lump sum

A single payment made at a particular time, as opposed to several smaller payments or instalments.

market share

The portion of a market controlled by a particular company or product.

minimum repayment

The least amount you can pay to continue servicing your debt or contract.

mortgage

A legal agreement by which a bank, building society, etc., lends money with interest in exchange for taking title of the debtor's property, with the condition that the conveyance of title becomes void upon the payment of the debt.

mortgage broker

A person or company that arranges mortgages between borrowers and lenders.

non-fixed bills

Bills that change often.

notice saver

A type of savings account. You must notify the bank of upcoming withdrawals in advance. Typically the longer the notice period, e.g. 30 days or 90 days, the higher the interest rate.

per annum (p.a.)

Each year.

principal

An original sum invested or lent.

refix

When you refix a mortgage, you are essentially ending the last fixed-term rate and starting a new one.

return

Profit made.

scheme providers

A company that performs all the usual functions of a superannuation scheme provider and administrator, including administering enrolments and withdrawals, allocating contributions and investing member contributions.

settlement day

The date a buyer pays the remaining money for a property sale and receives the keys to the property.

share market crash

An abrupt drop in stock prices, which may signal economic trouble ahead.

share

One of the equal parts into which a company's capital is divided, entitling the holder to a proportion of the profits.

side hustle

A piece of work or a job that you get paid for doing in addition to doing your main job.

split (mortgage)

Dividing up chunks of your mortgage across different rates and timeframes.

tax

A compulsory contribution to state revenue, levied by the government on workers' income and business profits, or added to the cost of some goods, services and transactions.

term

A fixed or limited period for which something lasts or is intended to last.

term deposit

A fixed-term investment that includes the deposit of money into an account at a financial institution.

topping up (mortgage)

Adding additional debt to your existing mortgage to obtain usable money.

unconditional (buying a house)

You are legally obliged to go through with the sale or purchase of a house.

utilities

Critical services to your home such as electricity, gas, water or sewerage.

Working for Families Tax Credits

These are regular payments for families with dependent children aged 18 and under. You must earn under a certain amount to qualify. Find out more on the IRD website.